Calla Hickox Burr
Memorial Fund

HARTFORD PUBLIC LIBRARY

His Life and Music

Neil Young

MICHAEL HEATLEY

Neil Young

His Life and Music

MICHAEL HEATLEY

HAMLYN

Editor: Mike Evans
Production Controller: Michelle Thomas
Picture Research: Jenny Faithfull
Art Editor: Ashley Western
Design: Alyson Kyles

Special thanks to Alan Jenkins
(Neil Young Appreciation Society)

Michael Heatley would like to thank Nigel Cross, who deserves billing as
co-writer for his assiduous writing and research against impossible
deadlines. Also Allan Jones, editor of *Melody Maker*, who was due to
write this book but in the event was unable to do so; his willingness to
open up the *MM* archives has helped immeasurably.

Nigel Cross would like to thank Richard Hoare, Colin Hill, *Broken Arrow*
(the NYAS fanzine) and Green Ray (formerly the Archers).

First published in 1994 by
Hamlyn, an imprint of
Reed Consumer Books Limited,
Michelin House, 81 Fulham Road,
London SW3 6RB
and Auckland, Melbourne, Singapore and Toronto

A Catalogue record for this book is available from
the British Library
ISBN 0–600–5841–7

Printed and bound in Spain

Typeset in ITC Fenice Light and Franklin Gothic No.2

Contents

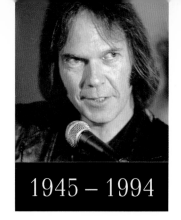

1945 – 1994

Introduction

When MTV unveiled a new concept called *Unplugged* in the early Nineties, it was all too easy to see the irony. The TV channel that had arguably done most to undermine live rock music by promoting the alternative idea of the promotional video clip was now purporting to 'invent' a new programme in which groups and artists were shorn of their electrics and effects, forced to return to pre-rock Fifties instrumentation and muster a respectable noise from the most basic of ingredients.

Neil Young had been at the forefront of those who'd poked fun at MTV and its 'achievements', most notably in the title track of his 1988 album 'This Note's For You'. Namechecking MTV boldly and directly, he'd sniped at the corporate sponsorship he felt was stifling music…and, in consequence, picked up an immediate airplay ban (this was later reversed, and – irony of ironies – the video clip he'd had shot to accompany the single picked up an award).

The rapprochement was complete when Young was invited to appear on *Unplugged* – and the timing was perfect, because not only did it follow the release of 'Harvest Moon', an album of country-flavoured acoustic songs that deliberately echoed 'Harvest', his best-seller from two decades previously, but when the performance was released in audio form it gave him a second commercial peak in what was the fourth distinct decade his music had graced.

Yet while groups like Seattle 'grunge gods' Nirvana, one of many Nineties superbands who'd cited Young's electric rock as

Left: Neil Young with the Blue Notes in August 1988, at the Pier, New York City

Opposite: London's Hammersmith Odeon, December 1989

a catalyst for their own experiments in the feedback zone, had to refashion their music from first principles, the Canadian could just revert to the acoustic style which had brought him success in the Seventies and Nineties. He had maintained a career on two fronts, producing electric rock with backing band Crazy Horse ('the third best garage band in the world') while embarking on rootsier forays with the Stray Gators, International Harvesters and other improbably named ad hoc groupings of musicians on the fringes of country.

This wilful eclecticism was what endeared him to fans…and frustrated the hell out of his Eighties record company Geffen,

Neil Young is the complete rock'n'roll all rounder, playing guitar, piano, harmonica and numerous other instruments, combining the archetypal role of the singer-songwriter with that of up-front lead singer in a variety of band line-ups

which tried to sue him for producing 'non-commercial music'! Indeed, the decade had brought a bewilderingly rapid change of styles with computers and synthesisers, rockabilly, country and horn-backed rhythm and blues with the Blue Notes.

If Young's music over the years has been dramatically varied in both style and commercial acceptability, his on-off alliance with David Crosby, Steve Stills and Graham Nash has never been anything other than musically upbeat and a roaring sales success. It reached its height relatively early in the Neil Young story – back in 1970, in fact, with the multi-platinum 'Deja Vu' album that racked up an astounding two million dollars' worth of sales before release – yet it was a phenomenon on which Young would deliberately turn his back. After finding enormous success in his own right with 'Harvest', his music became ever more bleak, personal and uncommercial as the Seventies wore on. Seasoned observers of his Nineties renaissance were heard to wonder if the current decade would follow the same pattern.

Young had earlier explained his depressing, doom-laden but nevertheless compelling mid-Seventies output by the fact that, having spent so much time (and made so much money) in the middle of the road, he now wanted to try the ditch! The period was dominated for him by the drug-related deaths of close friends Danny Whitten and Bruce Berry.

Critically reviled at the time, 'On The Beach' and 'Tonight's The Night' have since been re-evaluated as career highlights; in 1994, Mick Hucknall of Simply Red added 'On The Beach's title track to his own repertoire, a commendable recommendation in itself.

As for Neil Young, he simply goes on his own sweet way, both unplugged and otherwise. His last live performance in Britain at the time of writing took place in summer 1993 and saw him backed by the MGs, house band on innumerable Stax hits. A marriage of convenience or a pointer to future musical experimentation? Only Young knew for sure, and as usual he wasn't saying…

First Time Around

For most people, the image of a hearse is one of finality, the end of a life. For Neil Young in early 1966, however, it was the cheapest and most reliable means of transport his meagre resources would run to. And for Buffalo Springfield, the moment Steve Stills and Richie Furay spotted Young's sombre vehicle in a Los Angeles traffic jam was the moment a group was born.

Furay, soon to become lead singer and rhythm guitarist of the group, recalled the event years later. 'We were driving down Sunset Boulevard in a white van, and I saw a black hearse with Canadian number plates going the other way. I remembered that Stills had told me that Neil drove a hearse, so we chased him down. We persuaded him to come and listen to our arrangement of "Clancy". He listened and liked it, so he and this bass player decided to form the group.'

The song was 'Nowadays Clancy Can't Even Sing', and the reason Young's approval was sought was simple: he'd written it! The bass player riding alongside him in the hearse was Bruce Palmer, a fellow Canadian he'd played with in a multi-racial outfit called the Mynah Birds. They'd come south of the border to look for work after that group's dissolution, hoping to

meet up with fellow hopefuls Stills and Furay in Los Angeles – or, failing that, San Francisco.

They'd travelled more in hope than in expectation, Young's earlier meetings with the duo having been many miles away. Stills had met him while touring Canada with a folk group, while Furay had encountered Young in New York's bohemian Greenwich Village where he had been pitching songs to folk performers. 'Clancy' had been one that stuck in his mind.

The duo had been heading out of town when they were spotted. Some would call them lucky, others might say it was fate. Whatever, it was to prove a significant moment in the history of American music at a time when it was reeling on the ropes.

The British Invasion had all but swamped the land where rock'n'roll had made its first infant cries. Rock's first primal wave of Presley, Cash, Perkins and Orbison had inspired four young Merseysiders to pick up their guitars and invent Merseybeat . . . now the Beatles were giving a large helping of inspiration back to rock's birthplace.

Opposite: The legendary Buffalo Springfield: Dewey Martin (top left), Stephen Stills (centre), Neil Young (top right), Richie Furay (bottom left) and Jim Fielder (bottom right)

The Byrds had taken up their twelve strings in the wake of *A Hard Day's Night* and, like them, Buffalo Springfield would be a fab five: Neil Young on lead guitar the mysterious George Harrison, Steve Stills the ebullient Lennon and Richie Furay the melodic McCartney. The rhythm section of Dewey Martin and Bruce Palmer completed the line-up.

Childhood Years

A hearse may have provided Buffalo Springfield with their beginnings, but another vehicle was soon to play a part. Having practised earnestly, their thoughts turned naturally to a name. The one they settled on was found written on the side of a steamroller parked outside the house in which they were living: 'Buffalo Springfield'.

The West Coast was to quickly establish itself as one of rock's epicentres, where some of the Sixties' most exciting and

The Beatles at the time of the 'British Invasion' of the United States in 1964; they were to prove a seminal influence on the whole American rock scene for the rest of the decade

influential sounds were made. It was all a long way from Toronto, where Young was born on 12 November 1945 and Winnipeg, where he spent his teenage years after father Scott and mother Edna (universally known as Rassy, due to her dark hair) split up.

He'd been conceived when his father, then a sub-lieutenant in the Canadian Navy, was on shore leave, but missed being a 'war baby' by the narrowest of margins. According to Scott Young's memoirs, *Neil And Me*, published in 1984, the child used to 'jig to Dixieland music before he could even stand up for himself. His whole body moved to the rhythm; it was his unconscious parlour trick.'

Subsequent songs like 'The Loner' have led many to psycho-analyse his childhood. Young himself has since confessed to 'a pretty good upbringing . . . I remember good things about both my parents.' Indeed, the surroundings of his early years in Omemee, Ontario, where his parents moved in 1949, were probably much like any other Canadian kid's in most respects. Fishing in the summer and sledging in the winter, 'Neiler' (his family pet name) was visually identifiable by his dark hair that steadfastly refused to lie down and his ready smile – the latter somewhat affected by falling from a 'wagon' and losing half a permanent tooth!

His father's income selling fiction to magazines was uncertain, but Scott Young stuck with it rather than give up his rural idyll and return to Toronto and the staff magazine job he'd taken up when the war ended. Eventually, however, what he termed 'the strain of never being more than one step ahead of the bank manager' told, and he started writing for the then-infant American magazine *Sports Illustrated* – and ironically, given that the publication is now famous for its annual 'swim-suit issue' featuring nubile young models, Scott Young met and became involved with another woman while on an assignment. By this time, the Young family had relocated from rural Omemee to Pickering, an eastern suburb of Toronto, and for the moment remained together.

Schooldays

Neil's school record left something to be desired, his father recalling ruefully that 'he was not an easy kid to punish.' Brother Bob, in contrast, was a model pupil and, on at least one occasion, was deputed to accompany his erring younger sibling home with a despairing note from the class teacher. Music had yet to catch Neil's attention, but he was something of a schoolboy entrepreneur. One summer, when about 12 years old, he set up a roadside stall selling wild raspberries from a bush behind their house, a profitable escapade that led to him hatching, rearing and selling chickens. This enterprise was so successful that it brought his first serious ambition: 'When I finish school,' he wrote in one academic assignment, 'I want to go to Ontario Agricultural College and perhaps learn to be a scientific farmer.'

Neil Young's bout of polio at the age of six has been well documented, not least because it left him with a noticeable limp. But if physical weakness, if such is the word, militated against him becoming the archetypal North American sports 'jock', he was happy to pick up on music as an alternative that enabled the introvert in him to speak out. (Ironically, brother Bob was a gifted sportsman, excelling in both ice hockey and golf; he'd later become a professional golfer, and Neil would sponsor him.)

Earl Grey Junior High, the school in which Neil Young enrolled in grade 9 on his family's arrival in the city of Winnipeg from his native Toronto, a thousand miles away

When music first intruded into Neil Young's life, the gift of a plastic ukulele from his father not long before Christmas 1958 was the catalyst. The local radio station was 1050-CHUM (now CHUM-FM), and in time-honoured style he'd listen to this in his bedroom on his radio. His parents had an old Seabreeze record player, and it was the combination of this and the plastic ukulele that inspired his first performances. 'When (my parents) used to go out and leave me alone in the house,' he later recalled, 'I used to turn that old record player up to full volume. I had bought a couple of records the day I got the uke – I'd throw myself around, dancing, and I would have fantasies about winning dance contests. I'd always win them. The place where I won the most dance contests in these fantasies was the old legion hall in Omemee.'

Break-Up

With a professional journalist in the family, songwriting was the obvious next step. Scott Young believes that he may have influenced his son in his later songwriting. '(Neil) told me once that he learned from me that the most vivid way to get an idea across was to lay yourself bare in the knowledge that others would identify with the bareness, the sometimes painful truth.'

And there was plenty of that in store when Scott and Rassy Young finally separated; indeed, the episode was recounted for public consumption in the first lines of a song on his first solo album. 'Don't Be Denied' talked of his mother telling him his father was leaving: 'I think he's gone to stay . . . we packed up all our bags and drove out to Winnipeg.'

A second blow for the youngster was the loss of his brother Bob's company when he decided to stay in Toronto with his father. Neil had followed in his footsteps and taken up golf, but the presence of 'big Bob' had been a handy deterrent for any kids who'd been tempted to pick on him. Later he would have to fight his own battles, as he found on arrival at a new school in Winnipeg in the autumn of 1960. 'I looked up,' he later recalled, 'and three guys were staring at me, mouthing "You low-life prick." Then the guy who sat in front of me turned around and hit my books off the desk with his elbows. He did this a few times. I guess I wore the wrong colour of clothes or something, looked like too much of a mother's boy. Anyway, I went up to the teacher and asked if I could have the dictionary. This was the first time I'd broken the ice and put my hand up to ask for anything since I got to the f***ing place. Everybody thought I didn't speak.

'So I got this dictionary, this big Webster's with the little indentations for your thumb under every letter. I took it back to my desk and thumbed through a little bit. Then I just sort of stood up in my seat, raised it above my head as far as I could, and hit the guy in front of me over the head with it. Knocked him out. I got expelled for a day and a half, but I let those people know just where I was at. That's the way I fight. If you're going to fight, you may as well fight to wipe whoever or whatever it is out. Or don't fight at all.'

What the peace and love camp of Crosby, Stills and Nash would have made of all that heaven alone knows . . . but music was about to soothe the savage Young breast. The 'uke' had

V Records

X1-37
Jack
HARPER

V-109
Side B

45 RPM

"AURORA"
by "The Squires"
Produced by Bob Bradburn

long since been succeeded by a banjo and finally an acoustic guitar. But as the Sixties got under way, he found himself listening to the first stirrings of electric music. A fellow pupil had an amplifier, so he took the pragmatic course of action, buying a guitar and plugging it into his friend's amp. 'Then my other friend, Ken Koblun, got a guitar, a bass. And we started playing, you know . . . we just started.'

Young's early days would remain much of a mystery until the investigations of one John Einarson brought many details to light. He researched an article for US record collecting magazine *Goldmine*, published in January 1987, which eventually became a book and any account of 'the Winnipeg years' must perforce be indebted to his sterling work.

Toughing It

Young himself acknowledges that, although he effectively put his West Coast roots behind him when he used Toronto as a stepping stone to Los Angeles and fame, he owed much to Winnipeg beginnings. 'That's where it all started for me,' he told Einarson. 'There's no doubt about that. That was where a lot of important things happened for me.'

His first group, the Jades, was formed with schoolmate John Daniel whom he met at Earl Grey junior high school in the Fort Rouge district of the city. Daniel showed Young a few chords on guitar (Neil's first instrument being a Harmony Monterey acoustic with a pick-up on) in exchange for some impromptu golf tuition. The group played once, at Earl Grey Community Club, before a conflict of loyalties put Daniel in a quandary and caused Young to show an early flash of dedication. 'I had to go to hockey practice when Neil wanted to play, and he told me to choose one or the other.' Hockey won out for Daniel, but the youthful Young already 'knew when I was 13 or 14 that was what I wanted to do.'

Earl Grey was a tough school; how tough has already been related by the dictionary incident, and was later to be echoed

Opposite: An extremely rare single by the early Neil Young group the Squires, this was the B side 'Aurora'

Above: Kelvin High School, Winnipeg

by the references to 'punches came fast and hard, lying on my back in the school yard', again in 'Don't Be Denied'. His first serious band was the Esquires, an established band led by guitarist Larry Wah. The group even boasted a business card stating 'The Esquires. Instrumental And Vocal Styling. Fine Music And Entertainment'. Young sent one proudly to his father on the East Coast, but he was not to last long in the line-up. 'I was just playing rhythm guitar, and I didn't know what I was doing,' was his assessment of the period; Wah later claimed his guitar partner 'was so terrible that we kicked him out after about three practices. We tried switching him to bass, but he couldn't even play that.'

Above: The Squires in an official promotional picture, with (from top left clockwise) Neil Young, Bill Edmundson, Ken Koblun and Jeff Wuckert

Opposite: From September 1963 on V Records, a collectors' copy of an autographed single by the Squires, 'The Sultan' – 'Aurora' was the flip side

Next stop was the Stardusters, who were also known as the Twilighters. 'There were several names that we used,' recalls an understandably vague Young; 'I remember we had a girl in the band.'

There was a girl in the next band, too – pianist Linda Fowler, a member of the Classics which lasted from October to December 1962, playing a few Christmas hops before disbanding. Buddy Taylor played drums and John Copsey sang lead vocals, with Jack Gowenlock on rhythm guitar and – most importantly – Ken Koblun on bass.

Koblun's name would crop up time and again in the early chapters of Neil Young's musical odyssey. Convinced by his classmate's example that he could play too, he'd persuaded his father to buy him a guitar for Christmas 1961, and apparently learned so quickly that he was soon on local TV backing an accordion player in a talent show.

By the time the Classics made their public debut, the former grade nine colleagues had separated in scholastic terms, Koblun starting Grade 10 at Churchill High School (where the band played their first gig) and Young to Kelvin High (incidentally his father's alma mater). The Classics played their second gig there, but 'had trouble getting gigs because we weren't good enough,' as Young recalls, and disbanded four shows later.

The Squires

He'd clearly acquired the taste because, by January of the new year, he and Ken Koblun had put together the Squires. With drummer Ken Smyth, guitarist Allan Bates, and a shifting cast of supernumary vocalists and various instrumentalists, they progressed through the obligatory Beatles covers to playing a few of their own compositions at local dances. It seemed to be taking over from academic pursuits in Young's attentions: 'I used to spend my time at school drawing amplifiers and stage setups,' he said later. 'I wasn't into school. I was always flunking out.'

Early rehearsals were held in the cellar of Jack Harper, a firm friend of Neil's, who vied with him for early leadership. But sport claimed Harper's attention, as it had John Daniel before him, and in his words 'Neil really took control of the band then, and was the driving force.' Personnel changes around the core were frequent: 'We'd get different people and we'd change,' Young would later explain to his father. 'It was quite a way to grow up, you know, learning how to let people

go and then get different people . . . it's hard, still is, when you have to go to somebody and say, "We're going to get somebody else." Usually, when you have to do that, it seems it happens to somebody who's had the same thing happen before. The thing repeats itself. You always feel the rejection of all the other times, like a compounded domino effect.' It foreshadowed the sacking of Danny Whitten, and perhaps goes some way to explaining the fact that whenever Young has found sympathetic musicians he has tended to stick loyally with them.

The Squires got by on home-made equipment, Neil showing ingenuity by cutting his speaker cabinet at an angle for maximum sound penetration. The group's frequent rehearsals at drummer Ken Smyth's house culminated in blowing the speakers in his father's hi-fi set up, so separate amplifiers became essential. Occasionally, when playing bigger shows, they would borrow more sophisticated amplification from Chad Allan and the Reflections, Winnipeg's top band of 1963. The Reflections became the Guess Who later in the decade, and their lead guitarist Randy Bachman – who in the Seventies was a mainstay of Bachman-Turner Overdrive – proved an abiding role model.

'He was definitely the biggest influence on me in the city,' Young recalls. 'He was the best. Back in those days he was years ahead of anybody else . . . ' Young's hero-worship even extended to buying an orange Gretsch like Bachman's – though the reason was somewhat more prosaic.

'Neil had an old Gibson Les Paul Junior guitar that used to give him shocks,' recalls fellow Squires guitarist Allan Bates.

A very specific influence on the teenage Neil Young from the other side of the Atlantic Ocean was the British instrumental group the Shadows, and in particular their lead guitar player Hank Marvin (bottom left)

'One time we were in the Smyths' basement and Neil kept getting shocks . . . he just picked it up and threw it across the room and it smashed against the wall.' The Gretsch was soon acquired as a replacement from someone who couldn't keep up the hire-purchase payments on it, while Rassy Young bought her son a new amplifier to replace the home-made one he had been using. This, perhaps understandably, had given up the ghost as, in their drummer's words, the Squires 'played every church hall, school, and community club canteen in the city for two years.

Debut Disc

Initially excited by Elvis Presley's raw rock, Young had been reaching for ever more diverse strands to weave his musical pictures. Along with Bachman, one more unexpected one was to be found in Britain. He was Hank Marvin, the Shadows' lead guitarist whose twangy, tremelo-laced guitar lines had brought distinction to hits like 'FBI', 'Apache' and 'Wonderful Land'. Groups like the Ventures were much better known in North America, but Young preferred the more obscure Marvin, and indeed credited his influence – along with Randy Bachman – on the sleeve of 'Buffalo Springfield Again'.

Early repertoire for the Squires included the three Shadows instrumentals mentioned above – though Young drew the line at 'Cliff Richard stuff' – and other popular instrumentals such as the Champs' 'Tequila' and 'The Lonely Bull'.

By mid-1963, they were getting plugs and assistance from DJ Bob Bradburn at a local radio station, CKRC. That summer, the connection led to Neil making his disc debut as the Squires entered the station's primitive studio to cut two Young-penned instrumentals. 'The Sultan' and 'Aurora', both reminiscent of the Shadows, appeared on either side of V Records' release 'V-109'. Bradburn picked up the producer credit, though Young recalls 'a guy called Harry Taylor' actually operating the two-track equipment.

When it came to performing, his mother was an obvious role model, being a panellist on the quiz show *Twenty Questions.* Indeed, she took a keen interest in her son's extra-curricular pursuits, and though his academic prowess was nothing to write home about did not discourage him from a hobby many would have thought a distraction. Mrs Young became their unofficial manager, putting up the money to buy equipment like the Gretsch guitar. With its white case, this would survive until hard times in Toronto forced him to cash it in; he encouraged fellow musicians he encountered to sign the case, so someone somewhere has – knowingly or otherwise – acquired a piece of rock history.

Raucous Rehearsals

Young had been working hard at his guitar playing: quite how hard is illustrated by the fact that he'd taken lessons from a local player, but 'I found the guy didn't know as much as I did, so I quit.' He had moved with his mother from the first apartment they'd taken in Winnipeg to the top floor of an old house. This enabled Neil and Ken to come home in the lunch hour and practice, in addition to their after-school sessions. 'We played loud, for sure,' he'd later recall, 'and some of the neighbours complained, but we did it mainly in the daytime, not all hours of the night.'

His mother became adept at fending off the neighbours who complained about the band's raucous rehearsals, and didn't seem to mind in the least. Indeed, as Neil's brother Bob explained in 1971, she made something of a specialty of sticking up for the Squires, notably when a school official called to cancel a concert on the grounds that a mention on the local radio station would attract an unruly element. 'The goddamn fool told me all about camp followers right back to the War of the Roses,' she explained. 'So I told this idiot that if he wanted to cancel the dance that was all right with me. The contract read that the Squires got paid regardless, and I'd be right over to pick up the cheque.' Needless to say, the jobsworth gave way in the face of such righteous maternal wrath.

When permitted to play it, the Squires' repertoire now ranged widely, the instrumentals of previous months having been augmented by vocal numbers. Ken Koblun, who lived with a British family, had English hits sent to them before they had a chance to reach Winnipeg. Meanwhile, Young was preparing his own compositions, which he would get transcribed into sheet music by a female friend and mail to himself as a primitive form of copyrighting them.

They'd re-entered the CKRC studio in spring 1964, with Neil now officially lead singer, to cut some songs, including an original called 'Ain't It The Truth'. It's said the recordings were for submission to London Records of Canada, who'd expressed an interest in signing the Squires, but if so nothing came of it. Indeed, previously mentioned producer Harry Taylor told Young 'You're a good guitar player, kid, but you'll never make it as a singer.'

The house at 1123 Grosvenor Avenue, in the genteel Winnipeg suburb of Crescentwood, where Neil and his mother moved to occupy the second floor flat in 1962

Two Squires bass drum heads, made by Bob Clark for the group's first out-of-town engagement which was in Churchill, Manitoba, in April 1965

It was as noteworthy a gaffe as John Lennon's Aunt Mimi ever made; indeed, Young returned to the radio station years later on a visit to Winnipeg 'to show that you were wrong' (ironically, Taylor failed to recognise him!). His mother Rassy was a staunch supporter of the youngster's controversial vocal style. 'Everybody said Neil couldn't sing except me,' she claimed later. 'I said, "It's an interesting key, but if that's your key who cares?"'

The songs he was singing were stylistically widespread, the Beatles being the one over-riding influence. Allan Bates recalls one date at the Riverview Community Club. 'Neil got some really long Beatle wigs. We wore them on stage and sang some Beatles stuff, and boy, the girls sure loved that!' Other material ranged from traditional folk like 'Cotton Fields' to more rocky material like 'Farmer John', a song made famous by the Searchers which Neil was happy to revisit on his 'Ragged Glory' album almost three decades later.

Rock Dreams

But the lure of rock music was strong enough to persuade the would-be agricultural student to put dreams of farming on the back burner: in September 1964, Neil Young headed out for Fort William for a booking at the Victoria Hotel. The fee was $325 a week, food included – 'a good booking,' he wrote to his father. Come November, they were back there with a $25 raise, fulfilling Young's immediate ambition 'to get paid and improve ourselves'; other than that, 'I'm not particularly worried about where we go right now.'

By this time, the four-piece of Young, Koblun, Smyth and Bates was ancient history. The latter pair wanted to finish their twelfth grade at school, and Young, who now had full-time music in his sights, was not in the mood to carry passengers. 'It's too bad it ended on a sour note,' Smyth told John Einarson. 'We had a lot of good times together. To Alan and me, it was fun; for Neil and Ken, it was a career.' Piano-player

Jeff Wuckert and drummer Bill Edmundson now made up the numbers, though the former was not allowed to play out of town and the Squires became a three-piece.

It's often been recalled, not least by the song's writer, that he wrote the stage staple 'Sugar Mountain' on his 19th birthday in November 1964 while away on tour with the Squires. A celebration of youthful innocence that often appeared as a B-side but never made it onto album until 1977's 'Decade'

Chad Allen and the Reflections – they later became the Guess Who – with (clockwise from top) Chad Allen, Jim Kale, Bob Ashley, Garry Peterson and Randy Bachman

compilation, its chorus of 'you can't be twenty on Sugar Mountain' seemed to indicate an awareness by Young that the carefree years of youth he was now enjoying to the full might not last forever.

This was, perhaps, the happiest time of his life to date, being paid to do what he loved and discovering the country as he did so. Young's Buick hearse (his first car, which he affectionately named Mort) took them further and further afield as their fame grew, not infrequently breaking down and subjecting its occupants – now including drummer Bob Clark and a promising guitarist called Doug Campbell – to the indignity of hitch-hiking. It was in Fort William, Ontario, at a club called the Fourth Dimension, that he had his first historic meeting with another excellent young guitar player – Steve Stills.

The Au Go-Go Singers

Born in Dallas in 1945, Stills' first memories were of being in a car – undoubtedly not a hearse – travelling to Illinois. His father was a nomad, travelling from town to town making money, losing it and making it again. He was a music enthusiast, and the youngster had grown up listening to everything from Cole Porter through Leadbelly to the Everly Brothers, and had taken up the drums when only eight. 'My dad told me, "If you're gonna play music, drums are the best place to start,"' the recipient of a top-of-the-range Slingerland kit recalled many years later. Perhaps this early episode accounts for subsequent percussive influences in his music.

High-school bands included the Continentals, featuring future Eagle Don Felder, with whom he struck up an early partnership. 'He and I worked out a lot of double leads, like Dick Dale and his Del-Tones,' said Felder, 'and it sounded pretty funky. He had this drive. He was gonna go for it his way and be successful no matter what.'

In echoes of his father, Stills had travelled around the States seeking his musical fortune before gravitating to the New York coffee-house scene. It was here, in the Café Wha? where Jimi Hendrix would find fame, that he met fellow hopeful Richie Furay. A native of Dayton, Ohio, Furay had progressed from the local choir to a band called the Monks before packing his bags and setting off for the Big Apple to further his musical career.

The pair joined forces to form a vocal group, the New Choctawquins – soon re-named the Au Go-Go Singers – as an East Coast answer to the New Christy Minstrels (who featured a future star in Byrd-to-be Gene Clark, though no-one would then have guessed). The line-up was nine-strong, and included two girl singers among the 12-string guitars and waistcoated men. Among their first residencies was an off-Broadway stage production.

Understandably, personnel problems made such a large group a less than permanent affair and they split in mid-1965, though not before recording an often-reissued album, 'They Call Us The Au Go-Go Singers' for the Roulette label. Alongside Stills and Furay, the line-up for this comprised vocalists Kathy King and Jean Gurney, guitarists Nels Gustavson and Fred Geiger, banjo-players Bob Harmelink and Roy Michaels, bassist Michael Scott and arranger Jim Friedman.

Stills, who now 'wanted to be the Beatles' after watching *A Hard Day's Night*, went on to form Company (originally known as the Bay Singers and an Au Go-Go spinoff that included King, Gurney, Michaels – who went on to Cat Mother – and Scott). They embarked on a two-and-a-half-week tour of Canada which, although it made few headlines, was destined to change the course of American music.

Stills was immediately impressed by Young, with whom he quickly formed a firm friendship. 'We had a great time,' he later recalled, 'running round in his hearse and drinking good strong Canadian beer.' He even considered quitting his own group and teaming up with the Squires, but when the beer wore off realised the headaches this would cause. Work permit

Gerry and the Pacemakers (above in Liverpool's Cavern Club)

were typical of the English groups who conquered young

America in the middle years of the Sixties and had as great an

influence on US musicians like Young as did home-grown

rock'n'roll legends such as the Everly Brothers (insert)

The shadow of Bob Dylan's enormous originality inevitably fell on all so-called singer-songwriters of the Sixties. Stephen Stills, who was then very much a beat music fan, actually believed Neil Young was perhaps a little too influenced by the enigmatic bard of Hibbing, Minnesota

problems would bedevil the partnership whichever side of the US/Canadian border they chose to ply their trade, and it seemed destined to remain a pipedream.

Not that Young was hanging around to find out. He'd moved the Squires to Toronto – 'He wanted to go to England and play the Cavern Club,' reveals Koblun, 'but didn't have the money' – but the big city proved to be too much for the band, which had undergone a bewildering series of line-up changes in its short history. 'We sort of died out in Toronto . . . kind of lost our spirit,' Young would later reflect.

In the wake of Bob Dylan, whose early fame had inspired many a singer-songwriter, Young folded the Squires in the summer of 1965 and played the coffee houses as an acoustic troubadour. The theme of turning from electric rock to gentler acoustic folk and country would be a recurring one throughout his long career.

'When I finally did get hold of a phone number in Toronto and called him,' Stills later recalled, 'he'd gone back to being a folk singer, playing acoustic guitar in coffee houses, something I'd already been doing for three years. So that was it . . . Neil wanted to be Bob Dylan, I wanted to be the Beatles.'

Despite the support of a girlfriend, Vicky Taylor, Young felt that fame and fortune were still as far away as ever. Taking his fate into his own hands, he hopped down to New York with Ken Koblun (the latter more interested in chasing the girlfriend of Stills' bass player!) in an attempt to make some contacts and sing some of his songs to others.

'When we hunted around Greenwich Village for the people who'd been with the Au Go-Go Singers,' Young recalled, 'Stephen was gone. Somebody said he'd gone to LA to try to put together a rock'n'roll group. That was funny because at exactly the same time I was getting more and more into folk. Anyway, Ken found the girl and we hung out there for a few days. That's when I met Richie Furay . . . ' They'd never encountered each other before, but finding that they had a mutual friend in Stills the duo spent time playing acoustically together, and words and music were exchanged. 'I recognised Neil's talent right away,' Furay later claimed. 'He taught me "Clancy", and I started playing it at the Bitter End hoots.'

Returning to Toronto as his money dwindled, Young plugged back in again in the company of Bruce Palmer, another struggling musician who'd noticed him wandering around the Toronto suburb of Yorkville in the summer of 1965. Palmer, married and relatively settled though a year younger than Neil, recalls 'a tall, thin guy carrying an amplifier top on his shoulders and above his head. It was such an odd sight that I stopped him and we talked. Neil standing there with this amplifier top, going I never did know where. That's where we started this long relationship . . . '

Palmer had been playing bass for a group called Jack London and the Sparrows, but in a change of ornithological direction was about to launch the Mynah Birds, a rhythm and blues band that was named after a restaurant and led by the black guitarist-vocalist Ricky James Matthews. And when Tom Morgan, their original choice for the guitar position in the new band, flew the coop, Palmer recalled his recently encountered fellow musician.

Mynah Birds

It was an unusual situation for Young, who was used to calling the shots, but he took on the challenge and overcame an embarrassing first gig (where, it is said, he accidentally pulled his guitar lead from his amplifier in his excitement to solo) to become an integral part of the band. The other members, drummer Jerry Edmonton and keyboardist Goldie McJohn, would later hook up with singer John Kay and achieve fame as 'Born To Be Wild' hitmakers Steppenwolf.

During the day, he was pulling in a scant $50 a week working in the stock room of a bookshop. The orange Gretsch found a buyer in a music store on Yonge Street, Toronto's main thoroughfare; Neil now had a less luxurious 12-string folk-style guitar which, if nothing else, added an unusual new flavour to the group's sound.

And the Mynah Birds had a patron in John Craig Eaton, a member of the store-owning Eaton family who have given their name to Toronto's major shopping mall the Eaton Centre. Impressed by what he saw and heard, he bankrolled them for the necessary equipment, got them party dates to play and even let them rehearse in his home at times. Inspired, perhaps, by the backing of this embryonic retail magnate, the

The Monkees, whose Peter Tork (right) got the gig with the formed-for-TV group at the recommendation of Steve Stills. Legend has it Stills's teeth weren't perfect enough!

group combined folk, soul and rock in equal proportions and came to the attention of Motown Records, just over the American border in Detroit.

The invitation to cut an album's worth of material for Motown (unconfirmed rumours also suggest they released a couple of Canadian-only singles) was one they could not refuse, but wasn't the dream they'd hoped for. Supernumerary musicians were brought in to sweeten the sound, and anything the group had going for them was submerged as they moved along the famed hit production line.

Far from soaring to success, the Mynah Birds' flight was to be a brief one: Matthews, it transpired, was a deserter from the US Navy, and his recapture effectively ended the band. (He would later re-sign with the Motown label as controversial solo star Rick James.)

Buffalo Springfield

It was after this shock discovery that Young and Palmer had packed up the hearse and shipped out. (After Young found fame, Motown slated 'The Mynah Birds' for late-1969 release, but it never actually appeared.) Steve Stills had, meanwhile, been rejected as a potential Monkee – due, depending on which version you believe, either to his less than perfect teeth or the fact that he wouldn't be allowed to write songs. He recommended Peter Tork, a musician friend from Greenwich Village days, to take his place.

Other musical partnerships Stills is reputed to have forged while exploring LA were with idiosyncratic songwriter Van Dyke Parks and another duo with Ron Long named, perhaps apocryphally, Buffalo Fish.

Meanwhile, Richie Furay had been enticed to cross the continent from New York in the wake of some fanciful promises from his former Au Go-Go partner. The promising group Stills had asked Furay to join had existed only in his imagination and it had taken the Sunset Boulevard meeting to remedy the situation, all earlier attempts to build a group round the duo having resulted in failure. Stills had, however, managed to sell a song, 'Sit Down I Think I Love You' to the Mojo Men, who had a local hit with it; the song would later resurface on the first Buffalo Springfield album.

A local record producer called Barry Friedman had been impressed by Stills' work, notably with the Au Go-Go Singers, and had promised his new band work. 'He put us in a house on Fountain Street and told us to start working,' Young recalled later. 'All we needed was a drummer, and I think it was in two or three days that he sent Dewey Martin along.' The relief at being provided for after years of scuffling was evident. 'The whole thing was great . . . we had a place to sleep, and we could take a shower. We had a house and we weren't on the street. Barry gave us a dollar a day for food. All we had to do was keep practising . . .'

The initial nucleus, then, was Furay and Stills, but Young's arrival had created a new situation. Neil himself was convinced the alchemy was total: 'Three days was enough . . . it didn't take any time before we all knew we had the right combination. Time meant nothing: we were ready.' Symbolically, Young abandoned the hearse which by now was showing signs of wear and tear. 'One time when we got back into the hearse and started home, the drive shaft fell out into the street; we just left it there, unloaded our equipment and walked away.'

By contrast, Buffalo Springfield, the group not the steamroller, was showing every sign of roadworthiness – and Martin, the drummer Barry Friedman had located, was providing much of the motive power. He was the oldest of the group at 23 to Young and Stills' 20, Palmer's 19 and Furay's 21, and had an impressive pedigree to match, having played in the Grand Ole Opry band in Nashville backing legends like Roy Orbison, Carl Perkins and Patsy Cline. He also fancied himself as a vocalist, having sang and drummed on a number of singles with Sir Raleigh and the Coupons before joining electrified bluegrass band the Dillards.

'I hadn't auditioned in years,' he recalled of their first encounter. 'I was used to just getting a job and going to work. But I didn't have anything going, so I lugged my drums over to this old house on Fountain Avenue. They were paving the street, I remember. And there was this steamroller out front with a big sign on the front . . . When I walked into the house they were already talking about taking that as a group name, and I just thought, "Yeah, what a great name – Buffalo Springfield."'

The group played their first live concert at the Orange Showgrounds, San Bernadino, in March 1966. A residency that followed at Los Angeles' fabled Whiskey-Au-Go-Go Club in Sunset Boulevard put them in the spotlight, with the likes of the Mamas and the Papas, Barry McGuire and Sonny & Cher making the crowd even more star-studded than the stage. In

A typical poster in period (1968) 'psychedelic style', for the Fillmore and Winterland venues in San Francisco, advertising four Buffalo Springfield dates that also featured the Chambers Brothers and Richie Havens

The Byrds (above) and Sonny and Cher (below) were among the big names to flock to see Buffalo Springfield, then the talk of the West Coast scene. The Byrds gave them a support slot on tour, while Sonny and Cher's managers took them on

'Don't Be Denied', Young would sing of this period as 'businessmen crowding around to hear the golden sound'. The Springfield were indeed 'playing their songs for the highest bid', which started at Dunhill's $5,000 advance. Warners doubled the stakes before Ahmet Ertegun laid $22,000 on the table. 'I loved the Buffalo Springfield immediately,' said the Atlantic Records chief. 'There was something about how Steve and Neil worked off of each other. And all the members became very dear to my heart.'

Stephen Stills concurred. 'I remember that first week at the Whiskey, and the gigs we did with the Byrds. We could really smoke! The band never got on record as bad, or as hard as we were. Live, we sounded like the Rolling Stones. It was great.' For Richie Furay, too: 'The first six months that we were together were the best. Everybody enjoyed each other, depended on each other. We had these tunes, we had this desire, the shows were magical.'

Offers of management poured in: Brian Stone and Charlie Greene, who were already guiding the careers of the highly successful Sonny & Cher, were selected, while Byrds Chris Hillman and David Crosby were so impressed they offered them the support position on a forthcoming tour. The latter, of course, would play a major part in Stills and Young's future, while Hillman would later link with Stills in Manassas, so the Whiskey residency turned out to be highly significant.

The Byrds tour was followed by a bottom-of-the-bill appearance at the Hollywood Bowl under the Rolling Stones, after which Atlantic Records boss Ahmet Ertegun signed them up. Things were going right with a vengeance, and though their first single – almost inevitably 'Clancy' – flopped, despite Richie taking lead vocals instead of the 'less commercial' tones of its writer, the stage was set for recording sessions in September and October for an eponymous debut album.

By the time that first album was eventually released with seven songs written by Stills and five by Young it was clear the

Ahead of their time – Buffalo Springfield in classic pose with (left to right) Richie Furay, Dewey Martin, Bruce Palmer, Stephen Stills and Neil Young

pair had effectively assumed creative control of the group. Richie Furay had submitted one song for inclusion, but it hadn't been considered up to standard. Instead, he was allowed to take lead vocals on a number of the others' songs. Stills would later concede creative mastery to his partner. 'Back in the Springfield days,' he recalled in the Eighties, 'Neil's lyrics were far superior to mine. His songs were like poems in a way, while I usually got right straight to the point.'

For his part, Richie Furay – the man in the middle – had few illusions. 'I think they had me sing a couple of Neil's songs just to appease me, to keep me satisfied because I had all the songs that made it onto the second album written when we recorded the first one.'

Furay's 'My Kind Of Love' would stay unheard commercially until he formed Poco in 1968, while another song co-written with Young, 'Neighbour Don't You Worry', never progressed further than an acoustic demo. The same was true of Young's 'There Goes My Babe' and 'One More Sign', plus two numbers from Stills; everything else would appear on the first album, which saw Stateside release just before Christmas 1966 – any would-be British fans would have to wait until February 1967 for a domestic release.

Young sang lead vocals on two of his songs, 'Burned' (a first effort at dismantling the star-making music machine) and 'Out Of My Mind', while 'Do I Have To Come Right Out And Say It' and 'Flying On The Ground Is Wrong' were handled by Furay. Stills' highlight was the lilting, Latin-flavoured 'Sit Down I Think I Love You', while 'Hot Dusty Roads' revealed his blues roots. The album sleeve presented potted biographies of the band as featured in the rock press of the day.

Blind Date

Critical reaction to the release of the 'Buffalo Springfield' LP was favourable, but initial sales were disappointing. This was a source of frustration to the band, especially Young whose thirst for fame was probably greatest of all the members. Some consolation was soon to be gained, however, by the success of a single, 'For What It's Worth', which Steve Stills had been inspired to write by alleged police oppression on Sunset Strip. It soared up the Billboard charts to peak at Number 7, and Atco quickly withdrew the album to add the track in place of the same writer's 'Baby Don't Scold Me', a Beatle-esque rocker with comparatively slight appeal.

Melody Maker reviewed 'For What It's Worth' in February. 'A warm but mumbling performance from this American group,' it said. 'Interesting arrangement, very American guitars and English vocals. Could easily be a hit.' The following week, they allowed a reader to evaluate it in their popular 'Blind Date' feature, where previously unheard songs were reviewed without revealing the artists. Christian from Cricklewood (really) reckoned it 'more interesting and better'

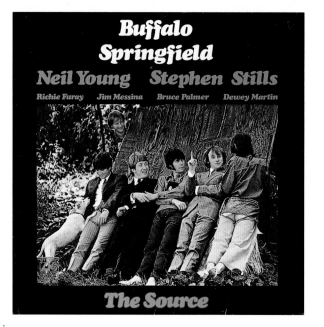

than Episode Six featuring future Deep Purple singer Ian Gillan. Despite this endorsement, it failed to chart in Britain where the group remained relatively unknown and unheralded.

Across the Atlantic, however, a hit single opened many doors, as the Springfield soon found when they were invited to open for legendary soul singer Otis Redding at Ondine's, a New York club, during his ten-day residency there. While over on the East Coast, they took the chance to utilise Atlantic Records' New York studio to record the follow-up single. Whether inspired by Redding or not, it was a song appropriately titled 'Mr Soul' – and, in keeping with the Springfield's quasi-democratic principles, Neil Young not Steve Stills was the writer.

'Mr Soul' is a song built around the guitar riff to the Rolling Stones' 'Satisfaction', and as such is not stunningly original in its music. Yet it's one that followed Young about, was reworked in electronic fashion in the 'Trans' tour and turned up again in 1993 when he played the MTV *Unplugged* show. The lyric dealt with the pressures and price of stardom – a comparatively new theme for Neil but perceptively written nonetheless.

And stars were what Buffalo Springfield undoubtedly were. Hollywood was the epicentre of the rock explosion, and many famous faces would meet and exchange musical ideas. Bruce Palmer later recalled the era: 'In LA the family got together. Day in day out we would jam together, be at each others' houses, just using society to make a rock'n'roll family. You got to know everybody – Janis, Jimi Hendrix, hell, we once even got together with the Beatles, sans McCartney, at Stephen's house . . . all those people in music . . . had a common bond.' But that dream was one 'straight' society wasn't always prepared to tolerate, as Palmer found when in May 1967 he was deported from the US after being found in possession of marijuana – a development that cast confusion over both live performances and sessions for the next album. His bass slot was filled by a number of people, including Love's Ken Forssi, Jim Fielder (then of Frank Zappa's Mothers of Invention and later in Blood, Sweat & Tears) and Young's old friend Ken Koblun. Since the Squires split, he'd gone on to minor success with folk-rockers Three's A Crowd whose album 'Christopher's Movie Matinee' would be produced by Mama Cass Elliot. 'I thought I was joining the band,' he later recalled, 'but they thought I was just filling in.' The sleeve of 'Again' dedicated the song 'Broken Arrow' to him, possibly as a gesture of peace from his friend.

Bruce Palmer, though neither a singer nor a songwriter, played a crucial role, as Stills later explained. 'He had a style with the bass . . . a Bill Wyman kind of Motown feel he put underneath everything, and it made it work for me . . . his relationship to me and Neil was the focal point of the group. He was the focus that balanced Neil and me.

But even with Palmer back in the ranks not everything in the garden smelt of roses. Neil was having problems with epilepsy, for which he started to take medication. He was also highly suspicious of the Springfield's new management team, who had bought out the formerly bountiful Barry Friedman. 'We never got out of hock,' said Young. 'They'd give us an advance and then when an advance came in from somewhere they got it. A lot of things didn't add up right, or at least we couldn't follow the addition.' It was this acute suspicion and confusion that fed his lyrics about the price of stardom.

Second albums are often difficult – and Buffalo Springfield's was no exception. In their case it was never officially released! A bootleg entitled 'Stampede' appeared later, though

Opposite: The sleeve for an Atlantic re-issue of Buffalo Springfield material, 'The Source'

Above: A vintage poster for a Springfield appearance at the Earl Warren auditorium in Santa Barbara, with the Watts 103rd Street Rhythm Band and the Lewis & Clark Expedition

31

Another poster from the Fillmore. Entrepreneur Bill Graham revolutionised rock concert promotion at the San Francisco venue with light shows, flower-power graphics and, crucially, in presenting all the new West Coast bands

it's by no means clear what the original track listing would have been. Among the Young-penned tracks that didn't make it onto 'Again' and believed to have been slated for 'Stampede' include 'There Goes My Babe', 'One More Sign', 'We'll See' and 'Down To The Wire'. The latter finally found official release on 1977's 'Decade'.

A cover photograph had been taken for 'Stampede' on which Dick Davis, who had deputised for Bruce Palmer on a TV show called *The Hollywood Palace*, stood in once more. It featured four band members in a suitably Wild Western setting staring happily at the camera, the fifth in a black hat apparently asleep: that was Davis.

The band was quartered for the 'Stampede' sessions in Malibu, where Moby Grape, another outfit that found greater acclaim in retrospect, had rented a beach house. The two groups hung out together, singing, boating and swimming – in short, anything but recording. (Young and bassist Bob Mosley would hook up again in the Seventies in a bar band called the Ducks.) Moby Grape were then dispatched to New York in disgrace by Columbia to finish their second album, the disappointing 'Wow'; Springfield started theirs again.

Creative Tension

Another reason for the aborted record was, quite simply, creative tension within the band. Young and Stills had rarely seen eye-to-eye, and as Neil's confidence in his writing increased he wanted more control over what was being done with his songs. This meant overruling Stills' talents as arranger, which inevitably caused friction, while Young's increasing willingness to take lead vocals brought Richie Furay into the fray. It all made for an atmosphere of confrontation. One redeeming factor of the sessions, however, was the recruitment of recording engineer Jim Messina, who would eventually take over from Palmer as the permanent bass player.

Young, however, already had one foot out of the door. His decision to quit came on the eve of Monterey Pop, first and arguably best of the Sixties' major festivals. 'I couldn't handle it,' he confessed later. 'I don't know why but something inside me felt like I wasn't quite on track.' The catalyst had been a booking on TV's prestigious *Johnny Carson Show*, success on which would have sent Springfield into the big league.

For Richie Furay, it was the last straw. 'I think Neil always wanted to be a solo artist, and I can't hold that against him. It just seems there may have been a different way to make that point clear rather than just not show up.'

Stills was equally trenchant about the incident. 'The *Carson Show* was like *The Ed Sullivan Show* at the time. It was an important show to be on in 1967. We were playing our best ever. But Neil quit the night before we were to leave for New York. It was sheer self-destruct.'

Having blown out the show, Stills was adamant that they would appear at Monterey, even though there was a matter of weeks to go. Recruiting Doug Hastings from the Daily Flash as lead guitarist, they worked him in with three nights at the Fillmore – then added a margin of security by persuading David Crosby, then best known as a member of the Byrds, to sing with them.

'I said I'd sit in with them to cover,' Crosby explained later, insisting that permanent membership was never an issue. As it transpired, his 'special guest star' status did them no harm at all – and, of course, proved to be half a dress rehearsal for the Crosby Stills Nash and Young teaming that would play the second great festival, Woodstock, some two years later.

Like Woodstock, the Monterey set was taped for posterity, though it was not until 1994 that it appeared legally in the UK on the Castle label. For David Crosby, the show would be an affectionate memory: 'For a grand total of 45 minutes I was in the Buffalo Springfield.' Fellow Byrd Chris Hillman remembers it rather differently. 'We got upset because one just didn't do

Albums were often packaged completely differently for various territories; this is the British release cover for the eponymous debut album by Buffalo Springfield

that then. We were competitive kids and it seemed like David was telling us, "Hey, look at me. I can play wherever I want".'

For Dewey Martin, the Springfield without Neil simply 'wasn't the same. We were used to getting a solo from Neil and a solo from Stephen. That was the unique thing we had going for us, the two lead players trading back and forth.'

But their triumph against the odds was not enough to rescue the year. 'All through 1967, the group was scattering, fragmenting, breaking up, coming and going,' Furay recalls. *Melody Maker* had reported an attempt to bring the Springfield, along with several other top West Coast groups, to London for two weeks' promotion and appearances. 'We are trying to bring the West Coast sound to the West End,' Simon Hayes of London's Saville Theatre told the *Maker*. 'We have

Above: Springfield gig at the Earl Warren which also involved Charles Lloyd and Turqoise; the legend that appears behind the figure might be interpreted differently today, it reads 'We have no souls and are gay without care'

Opposite: An ATCO (a subsidiary of Atlantic) release for the French market, a single featuring 'Rock'n'Roll Woman'

written to English and American record companies to help arrange a promotion deal if the cost proves too high for us.'

Along with Buffalo Springfield, the Saville Theatre hoped to import Jefferson Airplane, Love, the Doors, the Seeds and the Grateful Dead, and intended some North of England appearances as well as two weekends of London appearances. Needless to say, perhaps, this ambitious venture failed to materialise and as with Elvis Presley, the Springfield were destined to remain aloof from the British stage.

The following month, *Melody Maker* carried a report from US stringer Ron Grevatt that suggested the game was up altogether. Beside a picture of a beaming Louis Armstrong (67) and Herb Alpert (29), and under the heading 'Buffalo Rumours' came the following: 'The group have pulled out of the Gene Pitney tour, and Steve Stills and Neil Young are reported to be leaving. According to inside sources, there is unrest within the Springfield.'

The rumours may first have surfaced earlier in 1967 when, as Dewey Martin later recalled, the creative tension that fired Stills and Young's stage partnership boiled over off it. 'Things got pretty hot on stage, and when Neil and Stephen got into the dressing room they started swinging at each other with their guitars. It was like two old ladies going at it with their purses.' For Stills, it was also a matter of territory. 'Neil was trying to arrange some stuff, which was my trip, and I was getting more into lead guitar which he thought was his trip. So things got intense for a while.'

Harmonic Masterpiece

Back in the US of A, 'Rock'n'Roll Woman', a Stills song 'inspired by David Crosby', peaked at Number 44 in October 1967, as the second album finally emerged and in turn reached Number 44 in Billboard's album chart. In many respects, and again astonishingly given the circumstances, it perfectly encapsulated the group's appeal with its mixture of acoustic and electric instrumentation and keening harmonies. Furay's country style, Stills' rock and Young's melancholic ballads all fused to create a masterpiece.

That such a recording had been achieved despite the friction that was going on was remarkable: indeed, Stills had come up with a clutch of all-time classics in the shape of 'Bluebird', 'Everydays' and 'Rock'n'Roll Woman'. The question was whether Young could rise to the challenge of equalling those songs, though the choice of the already-heard 'Mr Soul' as album opener, albeit a different take, suggested otherwise.

The epic 'Expecting To Fly' confounded such pessimism in the most positive way. Constructed from two or three individual songs, it took, said Young, some three weeks to record and mix – surprising, perhaps, given the low fidelity of the recording. But this, he insisted, was intentional. 'The words . . . are buried on spots, but the general mood of the song is there . . . It's not like a modern recording, (it's) the Phil Spector idea of blending them all so they all sound like a wall of sound.' The song itself dealt with a relationship failing to achieve 'lift-off'.

Surprisingly, one fellow artist who didn't rate 'Expecting To Fly' at all highly was Steve Winwood, who reviewed the track in *Melody Maker* when it was released in Britain as a single. Guesting in the Blind Date spot, he identified the song as by an American group, but initially plumped for the Young Rascals. 'It gets a bit boring after the introduction,' he noted, adding that 'It's a nice sound (but) on first hearing it was a bit monotonous. We did a long fade-in intro once, but it can cause terrible hang-ups with the disc jockeys. Definitely not a hit.' If 'Expecting To Fly' impressed everyone but the Traffic singer, then 'Broken Arrow', a sound collage constructed with the help of arranger Jack Nitzsche, was Neil Young's piece de resistance. It was compared by some commentators to the Beatles' groundbreaking work circa 'Revolver', ironically since the screams were taped from a Los Angeles concert by the Fab Four. The title of 'Broken Arrow' – symbolic, explained Young, in being 'the Indian sign of peace, usually after losing a war, an image of being very scared and mixed up' – was potent enough to be borrowed and used as a title by the leading Neil Young fanzine, while the partnership between Young and Nitzsche was destined to be an enduring one.

'Expecting To Fly' was taken out as a single in January 1968 and grazed the Hot 100 in the States (Britain – and *Melody Maker's* readers – had followed Steve Winwood's advice), but the group was already destabilising rapidly. Neil had rejoined the band the previous September when Doug Hastings was dismissed, but though initial sales of a quarter of a million copies set them on the crest of a commercial wave things were not going as swimmingly as might be hoped.

Dewey Martin's view from behind the drum kit was of a band divided. 'Every guy had his songs, his studio time and his frame of mind.' Furay concurred: 'On the second record we drifted off into a lot of our own things, and a lot of overdubs were used.' It was all a far cry from their debut sessions for Buffalo Springfield. 'The first time we just set up in the studio and played, with a four-track machine going.'

The British supergroup Cream (left to right, Clapton, Baker and Bruce) were among those who regularly hung out with the Springfield, but a drugs bust in March 1968, which coincided with a visit from guitarist Eric Clapton, was less than welcome

The exception to this rule was 'Everydays' which, the sleeve noted proudly, was 'recorded live at Gold Star' with Jim Fielder on bass. Another curiosity was a vocal spot from Dewey Martin on Furay's 'Good Time Boy', which featured the horn section of the American Soul Train. Stills' uptempo 'Bluebird' was more of a genuine highlight; it was edited to just under four and a half minutes, the original nine-minute version later surfacing on a 1973 compilation.

'Again' received a critical thumbs up from *Melody Maker*'s Chris Welch in February 1968. 'Peculiar things happen,' he noted, 'on the American group's collection of original compositions and treatments. Heartbeats, jazz piano and rock'n'roll beats are mixed into a programme that demands intensive listening to gain maximum understanding and musical rewards.' After noting that the album sleeve joined 'the trend towards dedications, as indulged by Eric Burdon on his last

album,' Welch concluded that '"Broken Arrow", lasting six minutes, is the main freakout . . .'

Talking of freakouts, tensions were now developing between Palmer and Stills: the bassist was now apparently learning sitar and living in a tree house. They came to blows once onstage when, according to Stills, 'Bruce was playing so loud no-one could hear themselves . . . he slapped me across the face, so I went completely purple with rage and put him through the drums.'

Final Curtain

Young's future manager Elliot Roberts was now on the scene to witness the final, painful breakup. 'Stephen thought the Springfield was his band,' he later commented, 'but Neil had all of these great songs. I'd hang out with Neil up at his house and he basically had a lot of the songs that showed up on his first two or three solo albums. Yet Stephen and Neil had a great deal of respect for each other. I think that's why the Springfield stayed together as long as it did. But it was just a matter of time before it had to break up.'

Young was clearly at his wits' end. 'I just couldn't handle it,' he admitted later. 'My nerves couldn't handle the trip. It wasn't me scheming for a solo career, it wasn't anything but my nerves . . . I was going crazy you know, joining and quitting and joining again. I began to feel that I didn't have to answer to, or obey, anyone. I just wasn't mature enough to deal with it. I was very young. We were getting the shaft from every angle, and it seemed like we were trying to make it so bad and getting nowhere.'

Managers came and went in quick succession, and though Beach Boys manager Nick Grillo ended up in the hot seat personnel problems were now clearly almost terminal. The final curtain was hastened by a drugs bust on 20 March in which the whole group were involved: it occurred when they were jamming in Topanga Canyon with Cream's guitarist Eric

Clapton. Six weeks later, Buffalo Springfield played their final gig in Long Beach, Los Angeles, on 5 May 1968.

The third Buffalo Springfield LP 'Last Time Around', assembled posthumously by Furay and Messina from late-1967 sessions, was released in September 1968 and reached US Number 42. By that time, however, the members had already started their own projects. Stills assisted Al Kooper to complete the LP 'Super Session' before linking with David Crosby and Graham Nash, and Furay to plan the formation of Pogo (the original name of Poco), in which Messina would join him. Dewey Martin would attempt to form a new Buffalo Springfield six months later, but was prevented from using the name, and disappeared from view soon after.

Only two full Young compositions appeared on 'Last Time Around', though both were worthy of note. 'On The Way Home' (sung by Furay and weighed down by a poor brass arrangement) seemed to relate to his comings and goings from the Springfield, while 'I Am A Child' was a hymn to the innocence of childhood and seemed to be an answer to Furay's 'A Child's Claim To Fame' from the previous album.

It would remain in Young's repertoire for some time thereafter, while his other offering became the opener to his Seventies acoustic sets in what was by comparison a rather stripped-down form. (A third song, 'It's So Hard To Wait', was sung by Richie; supposedly co-written by Furay and Young, it had been completed by the former from a song snippet supplied by the latter.)

It was perhaps inevitable that the tracks on 'Last Time Around' should point strongly to the individuals' intentions, and echo the work they would go on to do after the break-up. Furay would revamp 'Kind Woman' in his next band. Neil Young's 'I Am A Child' featured the boyfriend of the Sunset Sound studio receptionist on bass, because he was the only other person apart from its writer around: as Neil put it 'we all cooked separately in the studios.'

'In The Hour Of Not Quite Rain' owed its lyric to a competition run by a teen magazine which offered readers a chance to 'write a song for the Springfield'. In the event, Micki Kallen was entrusted with the words, Richie Furay writing the accompanying music; the result was a lot better than it might have been.

Despite Stills' five songs giving him the lion's share of the Springfield's final offering, it was Young's 'On The Way Home' that struggled to the US Number 82 position when released as a single in October 1968. In Britain, *Melody Maker* gave pop-eyed cult comedian Marty Feldman a shot at reviewing the singles in June, and after slating the Doors' 'The Unknown Soldier' as 'over-produced . . . frantic', he reckoned the Springfield's 'Uno Mundo' 'swings like a bitch. I like that very much. I hope it makes it.' Needless to say, it didn't.

'We were good, even great,' Young summarised. 'I thought when we started we'd be together forever. We were just too

From the days of 'Mort' the famous Buick hearse, Neil Young's passion for vintage American cars was well-known. Here he is seen with a late Forties model Lincoln Continental

young to be patient and I was the worst.' Things were not made any easier by his epilepsy problems and the medication that accompanied them. 'I'm sure now that the way I felt and acted was mostly because of nerves, the seizures. It got that I didn't care, that I didn't want to make it with them. I didn't want to be a slave to the medication I was taking . . . I know I should have been happy,' he concluded, 'but in some ways it was the worst time of my life.'

An interesting perspective comes from Byrds bassist Chris Hillman. 'The point about the Byrds and the Springfield is we weren't garage bands, we came out of folk music, so the major focus was on the song. If you were going to get up in front of an audience with an acoustic guitar the song had better be good.' It's significant that Young has not disowned his early Buffalo Springfield compositions.

Break Up

For record company boss Ahmet Ertegun, regrets were to be expected: Atlantic would be deprived of a potential dollar-earner, though he wasn't to know that Stills and Young both and (again) together would shift infinitely more units than Buffalo Springfield ever remotely aspired to. Yet Ertegun's sentiments seemed genuine. 'I hated to see the Buffalo Springfield break up, but it was inevitable at that point because Steve and Neil had very different ideas about which way they wanted to go.'

In the final analysis, Buffalo Springfield simply contained too many diverse creative elements to work as a cohesive whole. The individual success of Furay with Poco, a group which blazed the country-rock trail for the Eagles and others to follow, Jim Messina as half of Loggins and Messina, and of course the individual and collective successes of Young and Stills was proof of that. And Bruce Palmer would return to the Neil Young story in 1982 as bassist in his 'Trans' band. But that was over a decade away . . .

Buffalo Springfield
(Buffalo Springfield)   1967

The track listing is the one on the UK release, which includes the single 'For What It's Worth' rather than the original 'Baby Don't Scold Me' which it replaced on American pressings after it became a surprise hit single in early 1967. Young wrote five songs, making his vocal debut with the group on 'Burned' and 'Out Of My Mind', while 'Flying On The Ground Is Wrong' (sung by Furay, as was 'Do I Have To Come Right Out And Say It') was as oblique as its title suggested. 'Clancy' was, of course, the song that Young had taught Furay in New York before they and Stills hooked up out west, while Stills reprised 'Sit Down I Think I Love You', the song he wrote for the Mojo Men. All in all, a pleasant if unprepossessing debut.

Track listing:

For What It's Worth • Go And Say Goodbye • Sit Down I Think I Love You • Nowadays Clancy Can't Even Sing • Hot Dusty Roads • Everybody's Wrong • Flying On The Ground Is Wrong • Burned • Do I Have To Come Right Out And Say It • Leave • Out Of My Mind • Pay The Price

Buffalo Springfield:
Neil Young, Stephen Stills, Richie Furay, Jim Messina, Bruce Palmer, Dewey Martin

Buffalo Springfield Again

(Buffalo Springfield)   1968

Buffalo Springfield's finest half-hour or so included two undoubted Neil Young masterpieces – 'Expecting To Fly' and 'Broken Arrow' – plus a remake of the earlier (and rather derivative) single 'Mr Soul', a song which would, curiously, follow him around a lot longer than either of the others. Elvis Presley's guitarist James Burton (dobro on Furay's 'A Child's Claim To Fame') and a pair of pianists Don Randi and future Young collaborator Jack Nitzsche were apparent elsewhere, but the only real clinker was 'Good Time Boy', sung by the drummer Dewey Martin and an example of band democracy gone wrong! Sleeve credits ranged from the two Hanks, Williams and Marvin, to Otis Redding and acid-rock heavies Vanilla Fudge, giving some idea of the eclecticism Buffalo Springfield's music contained.

Track listing:

Mr Soul • A Child's Claim To Fame • Everydays • Expecting To Fly • Bluebird • Hung Upside Down • Sad Memory • Good Time Boy • Rock'n'Roll Woman • Broken Arrow

Last Time Around

(Buffalo Springfield)   1969

The album cover told the story: a picture of the five originals, with Young turning his head away, a collage of memories in snapshot form cluttering the back. Stephen Stills dominated the sessions, musically speaking, with highlights 'Four Days Gone', 'Uno Mundo' (a near-hit) and 'Special Care'. Young fans will recognise 'On The Way Home', though not in this over-arranged, Furay-voiced form, while 'I Am A Child' deserves its place as one of the best and longest-lived songs Young donated to the Springfield.

Given that the band had played its last concert in May 1968, this was a very belated postscript, assembled by Furay and Jim Messina, and one to which Neil Young had little input.

Track listing:

On The Way Home • It's So Hard To Wait • Pretty Girl Why • Four Days Gone • Carefree Country Day • Special Care • In The Hour Of Not Quite Rain • Questions • I Am A Child • Merry-Go-Round • Uno Mundo • Kind Woman

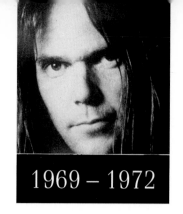

One Way Street

The final twelve months of the Sixties was to be year one for Neil Young the solo star. Perhaps surprisingly, it was not to be on Atlantic, the giant to whose Atco subsidiary the Springfield had been signed, but Reprise, the label founded by Frank Sinatra which was also part of the Warner Brothers-Seven Arts group. (Interestingly, by the end of the Seventies Sinatra and Young would be the label's remaining artists.)

The man who negotiated the Reprise deal was Elliot Roberts, a thrusting young manager to whom Neil had been introduced by fellow Canadian Joni Mitchell, an acquaintance from Winnipeg days. Roberts had already made an abortive attempt to wean Buffalo Springfield away from their management. Intending to buy them out, he'd been knocked back by Young himself, little knowing that the Canadian had already made the decision to leave the group for good and, only a short while later, would be knocking on his door as a solo star and potential client.

The record company's advance for the first album was quickly invested in a house in Topanga, one of the less fashionable Canyons outside LA where the Springfield had rented a house for a while. They'd been succeeded as tenants by David Briggs, a young Wyoming record producer whose career would quickly become intertwined with Young. The two met when Briggs stopped a friend's army personnel carrier he was driving to offer a lift to a long-haired pedestrian; in terms of chance meetings on the highway that led to fruitful musical partnerships, this strange vehicle was a worthy successor to Young's hearse.

The debut LP emerged in January 1969, – entitled, with impeccable logic, 'Neil Young' – with Briggs at the helm. It had been carefully constructed in a number of local studios with help on arrangements from Jack Nitzsche and a team of session men including guitarist Ry Cooder. Curiously, initial pressings had omitted to feature the artist's name (and album title) on the cover; whether by oversight or intention is unclear. But even with this omission corrected, the eye was drawn elsewhere. A burning landscape painted by one Roland Diehl in the style of Van Gogh flamed behind the singer's head,

A pensive Neil Young considers his future. Though he used his relatively rudimentary piano-playing skills to their maximum as a singer-songwriter, guitar was always his instrument of choice

the mountains above and a cityscape reflected below. And the content of the album was often equally unsettling.

Few could have been prepared for the contrast between the opener, 'The Emperor Of Wyoming', a countryish instrumental, and the final harrowing ten-minute denouement that was 'The Last Trip To Tulsa', its lyric 'Well I used to be a folk singer/ keeping managers alive' seeming to refer bitterly back to Buffalo Springfield managers Greene and Stone. If Young's material had spiced up the Springfield's albums, even a long-time fan might have found his solo debut confusingly eclectic.

The second side opened with another instrumental, Jack Nitzsche's 'String Quartet From Whiskey Boot Hill', while 'The Old Laughing Lady' which had closed side one would endure in the repertoire for some while. In 1970, Young would tell *Melody Maker* that it had taken Nitzsche 'a month to put down the tracks' for that one song – some indication of the complexity of the recording process. 'Everything was overdubbed,' he continued, 'to get that breadth of sound. But really I like to record naturally. I'd rather put the voice down at the same time as the backing track.'

The album's mix was a cause of great concern; Young's voice was far from prominent, suggesting a possible lack of confidence on someone's behalf. He was so unhappy with the result that he even proposed a unique exchange deal. 'I've remixed it and it's being remastered and reissued so that people will be able to hear it properly,' he said several months after release. 'And I'm working out some sort of deal with the company so that the people who bought it originally will be able to take it into a record shop and exchange it for a new copy.' Confusingly, although Young's remix immediately replaced the original US pressing, it was hard to tell which one you were

Emoting his lyrics with typical passion. Surprisingly for someone whose song words were always carefully considered, Young opened both sides of his first album with instrumentals

buying: since the catalogue numbers were identical, the only distinguishing feature was that remixed copies had RE scratched into the playout groove on side 1.

Sedate Start

For some reason this didn't apply in Britain, where every copy of the album was the original, accurately described by *Record Collector* magazine as 'sedate, low-key, with little variation of tone between instruments.' On the remix, the guitars and voices were given more depth and a couple of tracks ran longer before fading. Hardly earth-shattering changes, but clearly important to Neil himself. Yet even after all the palaver 'Neil Young' completely failed to dent the Billboard Top 200.

Nor did it dent *Melody Maker*'s collective consciousness enough to merit assessment at the time of release. The paper ran a joint review in September with Neil's next album, remarking of 'Neil Young' that 'its accent is on heavy rock and Young's voice gets lost at times' (clearly the original mix). 'Standout tracks are "The Loner" and the plaintive "I've Loved Her So Long".' The uncredited writer also remarked on his injection of 'more than a touch of drama into his self-penned songs', though by remarking that he 'recorded these albums between leaving Buffalo Springfield and joining the Crosby, Stills, Nash outfit' it could be wrongly concluded that this had been one of the briefest solo careers in rock!

Within six months of moving into his Topanga haçienda, Neil had found someone he wanted to share it with. She was Susan Acevedo, the strikingly beautiful manager of a local restaurant whose blond, shoulder-length hair gave her an 'earth mother' look – this being augmented by the seven-year age difference (she was 30, while Neil was just 23). The couple got married on 1 December 1968 and the picture of domestic bliss was completed by half a dozen pedigree Persian cats, a halfbreed husky dog called Winnipeg, and last but not least Susan's seven-year-old daughter named Tia.

A reminder of recent glories came in April 1969 with the release of a compilation LP entitled 'Retrospective: The Best Of Buffalo Springfield'. Including their chart singles, it equalled their highest US LP chart placing by peaking at Number 42. That eclipsed Neil's own effort, but things were moving at such a rapid rate that 'Neil Young', despite its recent release, was no longer really representative of the man and his music.

The process of recording the first album had been something of a debilitating one, as David Briggs recalls. 'I think all the thought and the work that Neil and I put into his first album, going from studio to studio, just made him tired to think about. I mean, for him it just dragged on – he's a really immediate guy. I remember after that, he said "Boy, I don't want to do that again, I want to get a band together and make band music and go in and do it."'

The next step, then, was to recruit that band. Young made the crucial connection when he dropped by the Rockets' homestead with one-time girlfriend Robin Lane, jamming on 'Mr Soul' among other songs. Although the group had only released one record ('The Rockets', on the small White Whale label in March 1968) they already had quite a history behind them.

The nucleus of Danny Whitten (guitar), Ralph Molina (drums) and Billy Talbot (bass) had been playing together since the early Sixties: Talbot and Molina, both New Yorkers, had encountered each other while singing in street-corner vocal groups. Talbot's family moved West to Los Angeles in 1963, where he hooked up with Whitten and Molina's cousin

Lou Bisbal. Their vocal trio was soon augmented by Molina himself, who was summoned from his new home in Florida to add a trademark falsetto.

Slick Act

Known as Danny (Whitten) and the Memories, they became locally famous in the Hollywood area and even cut a single, 'Can't Help Lovin' That Girl Of Mine', for Valiant Records. 'We were one of the slickest acts around,' Talbot boasted some years later. 'Really into arranging harmonies, the whole vocal trip.'

Moving up the coast to North Beach as Lou Bisbal was replaced by Bengiamo 'Dino' Rocco, they recorded a number of tracks as the Circle, with Sly Stone (then plain Sylvester Stewart, but even then an influential producer and DJ) at the mixing desk and providing the instrumental support. Then the Byrds hit town, and life was never to be the same again. 'We saw them in North Beach,' Talbot recalls, 'and realised right then that it was time to start playing instruments.' Molina had played drums in high school marching bands, while Whitten already had a guitar, so as Rocco dropped out Talbot, with few choices left, picked up bass and piano. They moved en masse to Laurel Canyon where they then became the Rockets, fronted by the brothers Leon and George Whitsell

The two faces of Seventies Young: grizzled and bearded (above) and clean-cut but long-haired (right). Few artists have rung the changes both stylistically and visually as often as Neil Young in what is now a three-decade career

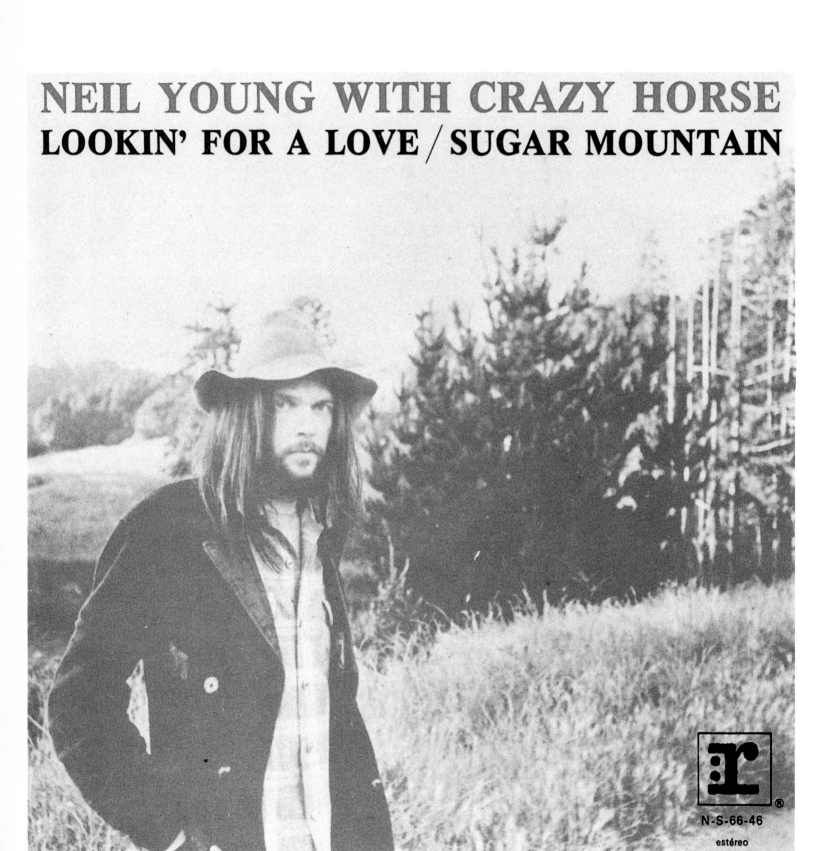

NEIL YOUNG WITH CRAZY HORSE
LOOKIN' FOR A LOVE / SUGAR MOUNTAIN

N-S-66-46

estéreo

and with Bobby Notkoff adding an unconventional instrumental edge to the sound with the electric violin.

Their debut album had pulled up few trees sales-wise, selling around 5,000 copies, but put down a marker – notably with the Talbot and Molina-penned rocker 'It's A Mistake'. The two main writers were Leon Whitsell and Whitten, with four songs apiece. Whitten's prowess had already led to commercial heavyweights Three Dog Night covering one of his first album tunes, 'Let Me Go' (their singer Danny Hutton was a Laurel Canyon neighbour).

Crazy Horse

Young needed a rhythm section, with harmony vocals a bonus, while Whitten represented a sparky guitar sparring partner, in the mould of Stephen Stills. Rechristened Crazy Horse, and with the addition of Jack Nitzsche on keyboards, Talbot, Molina and Whitten were to play a big part in Neil's musical future. And though the Whitsells and Bobby Notkoff fell by the wayside, the violinist made one last appearance with his compadres on the appropriately titled 'Running Dry (Requiem For The Rockets)'.

This track was featured on Young's second solo LP 'Everybody Knows This Is Nowhere'. Released just six months after his debut, it took a long time to climb to US Number 34 (earning his first gold disc), but included no less than three

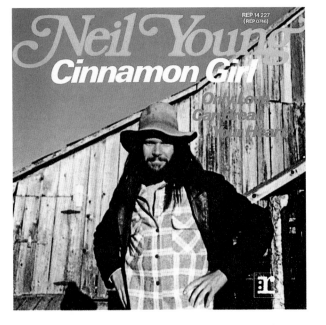

Left: While 'Lookin' For A Love' was issued as late as 1976, the B-side 'Sugar Mountain' was one of Neil Young's earliest compositions. Above: Released in 1970, 'Cinnamon Girl' was a first and triumphant collaboration with Crazy Horse

classics in 'Cinnamon Girl', 'Cowgirl In The Sand' and 'Down By The River'. Scott Young, in his reminiscences, claims these three songs were written in a single day 'when he was at home with a bad cold' after having sat in with the Rockets at the Whiskey. 'Cinnamon Girl' had been the acid test, Talbot remembers. 'Neil really liked the (Rockets) album, and he wanted to do his "Cinnamon Girl" with Danny, Ralph and me. So we went up to Neil's studio in Topanga Canyon just to work on that song.'

Despite the mere half a year separating the two, 'Everybody Knows This Is Nowhere' had emerged as a very different animal to its predecessor – and such contrasts were something Neil Young fans would have to get used to as his career continued.

Melody Maker rated 'Nowhere' a considerable advance on the eponymous debut. 'The second album is the best,' its dual review concluded, ' . . . using a relaxed and tasteful guitar, bass and drums backdrop with some nice guitar from Young himself. Three of the songs – "Down By The River", "Round And Round" and "Cowgirl In The Sand" are very beautiful indeed.'

Those three tracks were indeed highlights of both the album and Young's career to date. 'Round And Round' strongly featured Robin Lane on harmony vocals and was one of its writer's favourites, while 'Down By The River', a harrowing tale of love gone wrong, suggested that Young 'shot his baby' – a line he would later disown as metaphorical in an interview, suggesting there was 'no real murder . . . it's about blowing your thing with a chick.' The ten-minute epic 'Cowgirl In The Sand' closed the album, the critics unanimously homing in on it as the key track. It also contained the line 'has your band begun to rust?', introducing an image he would pick up on in a decade's time to greater effect.

In 1969, what was certain was that, with favourable reviews and increasing sales Neil Young had every reason to feel confident when Steve Stills came calling. He'd succeeded in establishing himself as a significant solo artist, and Young now found himself in the enviable position of being able to supplement that success by a brief and lucrative alliance. What was more, Crosby Stills & Nash & Young would give him the ideal platform to promote his own work.

'It was that June,' he recalled, 'when their album ("Crosby Stills & Nash") was just out and going like hell that Stephen came to the house one day and tapped on the door. He wanted me to play with them, not as a member of the group but to be introduced as sort of a walk-on guest, in other words a back-up. Maybe that's something he'd used as a compromise with the other two.'

Neil was rightly insistent, though, that he should have an equal billing: 'I already had a good solo career going,' he reasoned, 'and before I would join I wanted to make sure that the "and Young" bit was right in there.' According to his later recollections, that followed a month of negotiations: for David Crosby, less than full co-billing was 'never even considered . . . he was our contemporary, and a friend. And we never, any of us, thought of giving him any less.'

In a matter of months, Crosby, Stills and Nash had become a predictable and profitable hit act. In terms of following, they could boast fans from Nash's former group the Hollies, Crosby from the Byrds and Stills from Buffalo Springfield. Their eponymous debut album had reached Number 6 in 1969, won them the Grammy for Best New Artist and predictably brought demands from promoters for a tour. Crosby and Nash were happy to keep things acoustic – in Stills' dismissive words, 'going out as a sort of augmented Simon and Garfunkel' – but

Steve, ever the rock'n'roller, wanted the ability to rock out as well as perform more sensitive material.

And that was where his old Buffalo Springfield sparring partner came in: in addition to contributing a second dose of instrumental virtuosity, Young's recruitment meant Stills could switch to organ to add yet another sound to the mix. Stills revealed many years later that, while Ahmet Ertegun had been the catalyst who put Young's name in the frame, his own first choice for the role was Traffic's Steve Winwood.

'He was always my favourite singer, that blue-eyed soul sound. It had been our ambition from the start to convince him to join Crosby, Stills and Nash – I wanted an organ player who could sing the blues. He was exceptionally kind to me, but every time I trudged across the moors to meet him he was always occupied.' Stills had also approached the Butterfield Blues Band's Mark Naftalin, but somehow that was one name you couldn't quite see in lights.

Woodstock

So Young, not Winwood (or Naftalin), it was. And in a world soon to be bereft of Beatles, the idea of these four mega talents combining gave CSN&Y an irresistible significance. Both instrumentally, with Young and Stills crossing axes, and in the already fabled harmonies of Crosby, Stills and Nash, they covered all the bases.

Crosby hadn't been totally swayed by the idea of augmenting the group, as he admitted to *Melody Maker*. 'I resented the change at first, because I didn't want to lose that three-part vocal harmony, but it's grown into a fully integrated rock'n'roll band. Our music is going in every direction . . . one song comes out like Motown, one comes out South African, and one comes out like a Bulgarian harmony.'

Neil had played his first concert with Crosby, Stills and Nash at the Chicago Auditorium on 16 August 1969. Though he'd been asked to join the trio with live work primarily in

mind, as a full member his songs assumed equal stature in the set. Thoughts of committing this supergroup to vinyl soon surfaced, but first on the agenda was CSN&Y's second scheduled appearance: Woodstock.

However many millions of column inches it may since have inspired, Woodstock, 'the world's biggest rock festival' near the sleepy upstate New York village, didn't seem quite as earth shattering at the time. Woodstock's fame was assured by the film which recorded the event and took it to audiences worldwide. It attracted over ten times Monterey's 45,000 turnout, so given Young's reluctance to play there two years earlier it's perhaps surprising he deigned to show at all.

A ten-mile tailback meant that CSN&Y were helicoptered in to a small airfield nearby: that was one of Young's abiding

Young, Stills, Crosby and Nash – the dream ticket which proved too volatile to endure but sold millions of records for as long as it lasted. Until 1988, their reputation rested on just one superb studio album and some live performances

memories, along with an afternoon spent riding shotgun in the company of Jimi Hendrix in a borrowed pick-up truck. Neil was much taken with the guitar wizard, and in the Nineties backed up his assertion that the late guitarist was 'the greatest electric guitar player who ever lived' by bracketing him with another of his personal heroes, Hank B. Marvin of the Shadows, in 'Harvest Moon's 'From Hank To Hendrix'.

CSN&Y played on the Sunday, by which time the near non-existent sanitary and overstretched catering facilities had more than begun to take their toll. Rain interruptions caused the schedule to be pushed backwards, and by the time Joe Cocker, Ten Years After, Woodstock residents the Band, and bluesmen Johnny Winter and Paul Butterfield had done their

This picture sleeve of 'Cinnamon Girl' boasts an embarrassing early photograph of Young. As with 'Everybody Knows This Is Nowhere', the album from which it was taken, it carries a prominent co-credit for Crazy Horse

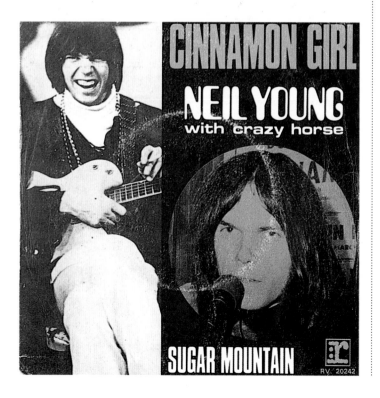

thing it was 3.30am on Monday morning. Crosby Stills Nash and Young, in their own words 'scared shitless' in only their second performance together, were warmly received – or as warmly as anyone could be under the circumstances.

Perfect State

Perhaps as a reaction to the subsequent hyperbole, few who were actually there speak of the event in glowing terms. Graham Nash claims 'talking about Woodstock is like talking about the Second World War.' For his part, Young declined to let himself be filmed; hence the inclusion of the acoustic set only in the movie that followed.

Hendrix, who played to 'only' the 30,000 people who had stuck it out to the bitter end, closed the festival – but that was just the start of the Woodstock legend. Two multi-album record sets were released by Atlantic Records in 1971 and 1974, while the movie – sold by the gig organisers to Warner Bros for $1 million plus a small royalty – grossed over $50 million and made stars of many of the acts who'd taken part.

Often imitated, Woodstock was never recreated. Four months later came Altamont, where Crosby Stills Nash and Young were also present and a man was stabbed during the Rolling Stones' headlining set. 'We let the Stones take that one,' commented Nash later of the 6 December date. While the Stones rolled on regardless, it dealt a death blow to festivals from which they would never fully recover. In all, two people died at Woodstock, but as a result of accidents.

Stills and Crosby had wanted to do the gig, but Stills recalled the atmosphere being so hate-filled that they cleared the stage 'in ninety seconds flat'. They were playing a second gig that night at UCLA's Pauley Pavilion; there, the tension caught up with Stephen Stills, who 'got the whirlies . . . an embarrassing end to a day best forgotten.'

As if refreshing his palate, Young had played with Crazy Horse at the Santa Monica Civic in November before rejoining

Crosby, Stills and Nash later in the month for the US tour that had included Altamont, and made it to Europe in January 1970. After dates in England, Denmark and Sweden he flew back to take up with Crazy Horse again as they rampaged up and down the US East Coast in February.

While in London, Young was interviewed on his own by *Melody Maker* reporter Richard Williams, and expressed his satisfaction with the position he now found himself in. 'When the Springfields (sic) broke up, I felt I couldn't work in a group context,' he revealed, 'and I certainly never realised I'd be in a group with Steve again, even though I guessed that we'd probably be playing together sometime.

'Now I think I've reached just about the perfect state. I'm part of the group, which I really dig, and I can also express

Above: America's Fab Four hymn the Woodstock Generation. The arrival of Crosby Stills Nash and Young on the rock scene filled, to some extent, the gap left by the now-disbanded Beatles, but ego clashes proved equally troublesome

Overleaf: Each CSN&Y performance would start with 'wooden music' performed acoustically, before an intermission. The four protagonists would then return, electrified – the reverse of MTV's *Unplugged* concept which Young graced in the Nineties

myself as an individual through my own things. And I need very badly to make my own music, partly because it boosts my ego to the required dimension . . . ' Williams didn't pick up on what might well have been an implied dig at the people he was sharing a stage with, but revealed that Young was to busy himself with two soundtracks, for *The Landlord* and *Strawberry Statement*, on his return, both films 'apparently products of Hollywood's new "low budget" thinking'.

The aptly-named 'Carry On' tour at the end of 1969 seemed to go on and on and on forever. *Melody Maker*'s Chris Welch caught CSN&Y in concert at the Royal Albert Hall in January 1970, calling them 'Crosby Stills Nash Young and Old' on the grounds that they faced the 'age-old problem of untutored musicians (sic) having to devote much time to tuning their instruments.' The unimpressed scribe, who confessed to dozing off during the acoustic set, was surprised at (or

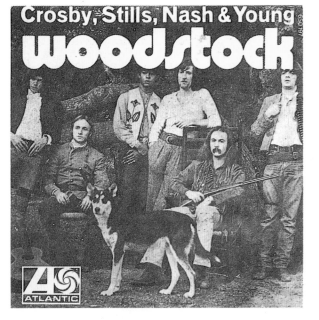

possibly woken by) the ovation a Stills piano solo received, 'although he had difficulty keeping time and seemed restricted to approximately three chords.'

Things brightened up during the electric section, during which the *Melody Maker* writer found 'Neil Young's haunted, lonesome voice with just the right amount of vibrato on "The Loner" and "Down By The River" was the high spot.' He went on to conclude that 'While CSN&Y did not deserve the critical

The album cover for Déjà Vu (left) quickly became one of the graphic icons of the early Seventies, the image being reinforced by re-use such as the French 'Woodstock' single sleeve (above)

pasting they received in some quarters, they could improve themselves by being a little less self-indulgent and knowing when to stop.'

Déjà Vu

But the whole wagon train just kept on a-rolling. If Crosby, Stills & Nash had made waves with their eponymous debut album, which by early 1970 had topped a million dollars in sales and qualified for a gold disc, the appearance of the augmented group's first offering, 'Déjà Vu', in April of that year was effectively the first major event in the post-Beatles era.

With pre-release orders in excess of $2 million, it became the year's best-selling American album, spent 38 weeks in the Billboard Top 40 (one week at Number 1) and confirmed each member as a superstar in their own right. It had reportedly taken about 800 man hours to record – 'ten eighty-hour days,' snickered Neil.

Drummer Dallas Taylor, who had also played on the 'CS&N' album, recalls 'You could never tell if it was day or night . . . we hid all the clocks so no-one knew what time it was. The sessions would go on all night, sometimes three or four days non-stop.' Young, for his part, remarked that 'Helpless' was 'recorded around four in the morning when everyone got tired enough to play at my speed.'

With four major talents coming together at Wally Heider's Hollywood studio, anything could have happened – and without the guiding hand of an outside producer anything did. If they didn't quite know what they wanted they knew what they didn't want: hence the firm rejection of 'Horses Through A Rainstorm', a song co-written by Nash and fellow Brit Terry Reid. 'In the end,' reasoned Nash, 'it smacked a little too much of the pop productions from which we had all just escaped.' The song finally surfaced on a 1991 box set.

Three tracks became US hit singles during 1970, buoying album sales through the year: the first, 'Woodstock', reached Number 11. Joni Mitchell's paean to the fabled festival that had represented CSN&Y's second appearance together was written purely from others' descriptions: she hadn't actually been there. Neither had Ian Matthews, who scored a UK chart-topper with it, but of course CSN&Y had. The group were augmented in the studio not only by Dallas Taylor, formerly from

the group Clear Light, but by the young ex-Motown bassist Greg Reeves who had replaced former Springfield man Bruce Palmer long before the sessions had started. ('He's into Indian or neo-Indian music,' Crosby had told *Melody Maker*.) Lovin' Spoonful leader John B Sebastian also dropped by to add on harmonica to the title track.

But reminiscent of late Buffalo Springfield, Young's two contributions, 'Helpless' and 'Country Girl', were cut solo

Young and Stills (below) and, opposite, Crosby, Stills, Nash and Young with legendary Fillmore promoter Bill Graham (on right). Both pictures were taken in 1970 at a London house on loan to the group from the Rolling Stones

before being presented to the rest of the group to add their contributions. 'He wouldn't let us have much to do with them,' David Crosby later revealed. 'He would cut the tracks himself, then we would arrange them vocally and sing them.'

'Country Girl' was nothing less than a three-part suite, consisting of 'Down Down Down', 'Whisky Boot Hill' and the title track. It was a major production number in the style of Jack Nitzsche, with whom Young had of course worked extensively.

He picked up another co-writing credit on the final track, 'Everybody I Love You', which simply welded together Stills' 'Know You Got To Run' (later re-worked by its writer on his second solo album) with a guitar riff Young had been kicking around in the studio. Neil brought other songs to the CSN&Y repertoire, notably 'Sea Of Madness' (recorded for posterity on the 'Woodstock' triple album), 'Birds' (a first album outtake), 'Everybody's Alone' and 'When You Dance I Can Really Love'. All were attempted during the 'Déjà Vu' sessions but, with four songwriters competing, failed to make the cut.

Of the others' contributions, Crosby had written his 'Long Time Gone' and 'Almost Cut My Hair' on the night Robert Kennedy died. The whole mood of the album was up, a true celebration of the hippie dream: only Young's two solo compositions and Stills' brooding '4+20' stuck out from the general mood. Yet Young would soon find himself infused by his colleagues' radicalism.

Of the other singles, both were written by Nash: 'Teach Your Children' featuring the Grateful Dead's Jerry Garcia on rudimentary pedal steel guitar, reached Number 16 while 'Our House', a somewhat sentimental paean to his then-current domestic bliss with Joni Mitchell, went to Number 30. In the 1990s, it was resuscitated in Britain (where the album reached the Top 5 soon after release) for use in a television commercial for building societies!

Under the headline 'CSN and Y – more guts, less beauty', *Melody Maker* hailed 'Déjà Vu' as 'Possibly the most eagerly

awaited set since the Band's second album, and contrary to some reports it's no disappointment. The only dud,' it wrote, 'is Joni Mitchell's "Woodstock", a dull song with rather messy production. But it's difficult to knock an album which communicates so well the solid pleasure of good musicians playing simple, honest music together.'

'Déjà Vu's optimism was very much at variance with the events of Vietnam and the Draft. And the violence of 4 May 1970 at Kent State University brought matters even closer to home when US National Guardsmen killed four students protesting against the conflict in south-east Asia. It shocked Young, who was inspired to respond in song. This was 'Ohio' which, released as a single just days later, itself drew fire from high places when Vice President Spiro Agnew denounced rock music generally as being 'anti-US'. As the news of the tragedy broke, Young and Crosby were staying with road

manager Leo Makota in Pecadero, a small coastal village 30 miles south of San Francisco. A heated discussion ended with Young withdrawing from the proceedings and picking up his guitar: 'Ohio' was the result.

Crosby and Young rendezvoused at the Record Plant in Los Angeles with Nash and Stills, who'd flown in from England. Bassist Fuzzy Samuels and drummer John Barbata, formerly of the Turtles, made up the numbers (though Crosby had nominated Russ Kunkel). The session moved Crosby to tears, as the end result did many listeners. Young himself nominated 'Ohio' as his best ever CSN&Y cut in his liner notes to 'Decade' in 1977, adding: 'It's still hard to believe I had to write this song. It's still ironic that I capitalised on the death of these American students. Probably the biggest lesson learned at an American place of learning.'

For Crosby, Kent State was the last straw for a usually mild-mannered colleague, one he would defend against charges of cheap sloganeering. 'I don't think musicians should go and seek stands out,' he blustered, 'but when something slaps you in the face personally you have to respond to it . . . Even Neil couldn't stand it. He had to respond . . . it was as genuine and honest a thing as you could ask for.'

Despite an airplay ban, the single rose to Number 14 in the US chart, backed with chilling appropriateness (and in echoes of Buffalo Springfield's quasi-democratic writing policy) with a live version of Stills' 'Find The Cost Of Freedom'. By June, the fruits of Young's earlier labours were becoming apparent. 'Cinnamon Girl', from 'Everybody Knows . . .' had risen to Number 55 in the wake of CSN&Y's popularity.

His perspective on the differing and sometime conflicting demands of CSN&Y and Crazy Horse make interesting reading.

Another guitar showdown between Stills and Young. Live recordings on the 'Four Way Street' album were elongated by free-form soloing that some loved and others found tedious

'I'm oversimplifying, but you could compare CSN&Y to the Beatles and Crazy Horse to the Stones,' he said. 'With Crazy Horse, I'm trying to make records that are not necessarily hits, but which people will listen to for a long time.' As fate would have it, it would be 18 years before he and the band released a new vinyl collaboration.

Writing on the Wall

CSN&Y had not enjoyed universal acclaim from the critics, despite the public's enthusiasm. Even by June 1970 the writing was on the wall – or at least in the *Melody Maker* news pages – for the quartet. 'How long can they survive?' wailed the headline, as the paper's Hollywood reporter listed three crucial 'facts' to support the 'rumours of the demise of Crosby Stills Nash and Young (that) have been circulating since the group's formation last year.'

These facts were as follows: the cancellation of a week's worth of dates due to Graham Nash's throat condition, Neil Young walking off stage 'in the middle of a performance with no explanation given' and the previously noted replacement of the 'Déjà Vu' rhythm section of Taylor and Reeves, which had happened in Denver. The tour did in fact resume, while an unnamed spokesman for the group insisted they'd fulfil their contract with a studio album once they came off the road. 'I don't know why they book a tour like that,' he continued in a somewhat less than loyal tone. 'The group doesn't need that kind of pressure. It's no secret that they're the top group in the country . . . they sold out six nights at the Fillmore East in just one afternoon . . . so they don't really have to kill themselves for the bread.'

The first of those Fillmore dates were witnessed by *Melody Maker*'s Vicki Wickham, later to become Dusty Springfield's manager. She was bowled over by 'a week of totally sold-out concerts, the only show I've ever seen there with the stage filled with flowers instead of a light show, and a genuine

neil young
old man / the needle and the damage done

'Old Man', the reflective second single from 'Harvest', was in fact written about a worker on Young's ranch – not his father

unhyped 15-minutes-plus standing ovation at the end which lasted through the house lights being turned on and literally forced them back on stage for a final finale of "Woodstock".'

Young's acoustic offerings included the yet to be released 'Only Love Will Break Your Heart', plus the well-known 'Down By The River', which he confessed he'd 'never done this way before'. 'If it's a good song, it doesn't matter how you do it,' said a supportive Nash as they all took turn and turn about.

They clearly felt the strain of the tour, but were determined to make light of the bad publicity. 'We broke up last week,' announced Nash. 'That's why we're here.' 'Yeah, and the Byrds broke up 74 times,' announced ex-Byrd David Crosby to ironic chuckles all round.

If touring to excess persuaded the music press that CSN&Y were cashing in, it was an ill wind that blew Neil Young his greatest solo success to date. By happy coincidence, the

Young with a Gretsch semi-acoustic guitar similar to one his mother bought him while he was struggling to make his name in the Squires. That was sold, but his love for the marque lived on

release of Young's third solo LP 'After The Goldrush' had accompanied this continuous touring with CSN&Y and ensured the album hit Number 8; in Britain, it went one better.

After the Goldrush

'Goldrush' had been intended to feature Crazy Horse, but Danny Whitten's escalating heroin habit caused an angry Young to abort sessions in favour of taking matters in-house – literally. Hiring a mixing desk and transporting it to his home, he reconvened at home with new personnel. Members of Crazy Horse were gradually allowed back into proceedings, starting with drummer Ralph Molina. Steve Stills contributed backing vocals from his current crew. But the most important addition was youthful guitarist/pianist Nils Lofgren who'd first met Young when he played Washington's Cellar Door club. 'I didn't know much about Neil,' he later confessed, 'apart from the fact that he was once in the Buffalo Springfield . . . but I thought I had some good songs so I played him some tunes and he liked them. I'd never really heard his songs, but our writing was very similar in many ways.' Lofgren hung around with Young, who bought him 'cokes and hamburgers', later showing up to lend him support when he recorded Grin's eponymous 1971 debut.

Having seen what Lofgren could do in the studio, his was one of the first names Young came up with after sacking his regular band. But in a typically unexpected move, he wanted the teenager – also adept at the accordion – to play piano. Undaunted, Lofgren practised for a couple of days at the house of Spirit keyboard player John Locke before venturing Topanga-wards. 'Neil was right about the piano,' he later admitted. 'He knew I played accordion and the right hand work is the same, so all I had to do was get my left hand together. He wanted a plain, simple style – and it worked.'

Young's previous albums had been as unalike as chalk and cheese – the multi-overdubbed 'Neil Young' and the loose, group-recorded 'Everybody Knows . . . .'. 'After The Goldrush' was deftly pieced together from songs and musicians old and new, rather in the manner of the patched-up seat of Neil's jeans, a picture of which adorned the album's back cover: this feat of needlework was credited, incidentally, to Susan Young!

The title had come from a projected movie by actor Dean Stockwell, the plot of which was based on a tidal wave hitting Topanga Canyon! Ironically, Neil would soon be moving to a ranch in San Mateo County, the other side of San Francisco Airport – but meanwhile, the concept of unharnessed nature certainly played a part in inspiring the album's title track if not the entire project.

That title track, crooned in a somewhat off-key fashion by Young to his own piano backing, would become an unlikely British hit single – not for him, however, but a cover version by harmony vocal group Prelude. They dispensed with the ivories, corrected the imperfect pitching and turned it into something of an ecological hymn on release in early 1974 (it re-charted eight years later).

Back at the ranch, Crazy Horse effectively reconvened for 'When You Dance I Can Really Love', one of the songs tried but rejected for 'Déjà Vu' on which sometime collaborator Jack Nitzsche played piano. As perhaps the most directly compara-ble cut to the preceding album, it was released as a single in April 1971 but stalled at US Number 93. The more airplay-friendly 'Only Love Can Break Your Heart', a song written for former confederate Graham Nash, had earlier peaked at US Number 33 – Young's first Top 40 single.

'Southern Man' continued the political edge that had informed 'Ohio', and has become Young's most controversial song to date. In its time it has inspired righteous indignation (most notably an 'answer' from Southern rockers Lynyrd Skynyrd in 'Sweet Home Alabama') and fan fervour. It was later all but disowned by its writer after a violent incident at the Oakland Coliseum during the 'Time Fades Away' tour.

'After the Goldrush' was Neil Young's most acclaimed solo album to date, being voted collectively as their Album of the Year by *Melody Maker* writers

Of the songs that had earlier been recorded for the album with Crazy Horse only Don Gibson's maudlin country lament 'Oh Lonesome Me' actually made it onto the finished release. (British singer-songwriter Al Stewart, listening to this in *Melody Maker*'s Blind Date feature, claimed it was 'Just some-one saying "let's find a different way of doing it" . . . trying to be commercial.' Numbers like 'I Need Her Love To Get By', 'Wondering', 'Big Waves', 'Winterlong', 'It Might Have Been' and 'Everybody's Alone' would remain unheard. This was to be a continuing thread in the Neil Young story – songs that, to all but the fortunate few, would remain mere titles.

The speed at which it had been done was, recalls Nils Lofgren, somewhat disconcerting for his boss. 'We would play through a song about four times to learn it, with all live vocals in the same room. In four days, he had written six new songs.

In fact, the whole thing was on tape in under a week allowing another week or two for mixing.' In the final analysis, Lofgren relates, Young 'liked the concept behind the songs but it had been done so quick that he was not sure how the public would take to it. He wasn't sure if there was enough in it.'

Yet it was an album its creator, in the final analysis, came to appreciate added up to far more than the sum of its parts. '"After The Goldrush" was the spirit of Topanga Canyon,' he told *Rolling Stone* in 1975. 'It seemed like I realised that I'd gotten somewhere.'

Imperfect but Irresistible

Melody Maker hailed 'Goldrush' as 'Imperfect, irresistible Neil Young': their assistant editor Richard Williams highlighted the fact that British critical reaction had been muted in the wake of supergroup hype. 'I've yet to read a really complimentary review of it, yet I know scores of people who've almost worn out their imported copies already.' Stylistically, he said, 'it lies somewhere between the first and the second albums: the arranged tightness of the first is mingled with some of the jamming spirit of the second, and in some cases the result is an ideal blend.' His highlight was 'Don't Let It Bring You Down', 'a song with the most typical Young minor cadences and trembling vocal line.'

Little wonder, then, that *Melody Maker* writers made 'Goldrush' their Album of the Year. Another fan, perhaps surprisingly, was teen star in waiting Marc Bolan, leader of Tyrannosaurus Rex. 'The album is incredible,' he told *MM* when reviewing 'Only Love Can Break Your Heart'. 'In America he is a giant, but in this country he's not so well known.'

Back in the USA, Neil Young was clearly a high-profile performer in his own right as well as with friends: on 4 December 1970 he sold out New York's Carnegie Hall twice over (an ebullient Jack Nicholson among the backstage revellers), a career highlight his parents attended though at different shows. The engagement was a solo one (the sold out banners adorned posters simply stating 'Neil Young: Folk Singer') and he switched between two acoustic guitars and piano with a slightly apologetic air: this was due to the fact that he'd strained his back lifting slabs of walnut panelling while renovating his ranch, an injury that would dog him for the next two years. He declined anything more than temporary hospital treatment and uncomplainingly fulfilled the gigs in a back brace worn under his clothes.

Even though 'Goldrush' was bound for a Top 10 position, Young chose to premiere a number of new songs in the set, including 'Journey Through The Past', 'Old Man' and 'The Needle And The Damage Done'. The crowd were boisterous and wanted their favourites, but Neil admonished them in kindly fashion. 'You don't think I'd come to Carnegie Hall without planning? You're going to get all the songs you want to hear.' He also poked fun at his rudimentary piano-playing when the introduction to his songs received rapturous applause. 'Y'know about these piano intros: I don't play so good. They're all the same intro . . . I just wanted to let you know that I know.'

It was a double-edged barb. But the audience were clearly prepared to applaud his every move – and never more so than on 6 January 1971, when Young returned to Canada to perform at the Queen Elizabeth Theatre, Vancouver. He then crossed the continent to Toronto's Massey Hall, selling it out twice in contrast with his last concert there two years earlier when, as a new solo artist, he'd only half-filled the small Riverboat club. Many of the people there then were friends from his scuffling days, and many were backstage in '71 to share in his latest triumphant homecoming.

'After The Goldrush' soared to sales success on the back of CSN&Y's corporate activities, establishing Young as darling of the singer-songwriter set

NEIL YOUNG

AFTER THE GOLD RUSH

r

NEW ALBUM ON WARNER-REPRISE

When you buy this Album at your Record Shop showing the sign

you will receive a free **Neil Young Poster**

He stopped off in Nashville to guest on a Johnny Cash show and cut a few songs for his next album, then flew to London for a 27 February date at the Royal Festival Hall. Queues formed by the Thames, waiting overnight to snap up nearly 3,000 tickets for which twice that number had applied: no wonder *Melody Maker* hailed him as 'the most sought-after solo star since Bob Dylan'! (Readers went even further later in the year, voting him top male singer: Dylan, the previous year's top dog when Young had been tenth, trailed in eighth place . . .)

Not that success was going to his head – in fact it didn't seem to fit securely on his stooped shoulders at all. An amusing anecdote was supplied by Allan McDougall, reporter with *MM*'s rival *New Musical Express*. Having hitched a lift from the airport in Young's limousine, he was still there when the car drew up outside some exclusive flats adjacent to the American Embassy in Grosvenor Square. 'The doorman, considerably more resplendently dressed than Neil, stepped to the kerb and said, "Welcome, sir. Your neighbours here are King Hussein, Raquel Welch, and Michael Caine." Whereupon Neil stepped back into the limousine and asked to be taken somewhere else.'

He put aside such feelings when working with the London Symphony Orchestra on two songs which would turn up on 'Harvest': 'There's A World' and 'A Man Needs A Maid'. David Meecham conducted them through Jack Nitzsche's arrangements in the long-way-from-Hollywood environs of Barking Town Hall in East London. His father Scott recalls him showing 'traces of the kid from Omemee, not realising how big he had become . . . "They were really into it, Dad. They treated me like somebody." '

The bedsit bard tunes up. Along with the likes of Cat Stevens and Joni Mitchell, Young's introspective compositions sung to softly strummer acoustic guitars hit a chord with many

Originally conceived as Crosby Stills Nash and sideman, CSN&Y found room for Young's compositional talents as well as his undoubted instrumental prowess

Opposite: The studio recording of 'Ohio' (reprised live on 'Four Way Street') was cut as a response to the Kent State shootings and was thus unavailable on album for some years

Four Way Street

Like the classical musicians he'd worked with, Young's audience, too, thought he was somebody. *Melody Maker* reported the Festival Hall gig as being the most important event since Bob Dylan in 1965 – though whereas 'the old Dylan was magnetic, hypnotic, a far-away figure who mesmerised, Neil Young was an old friend come to sing us a few songs. The sense of occasion, so strong that it almost curled into the nostrils, was created not by the performer but by the audience and their expectations.'

As some consolation to those who had been unable to squeeze into the Festival Hall, Young recorded a show for BBC2's acclaimed *In Concert* series. And though the TV studio could only hold 240 people (despite a postal strike, the BBC ticket unit could have disposed of ten times the number of tickets), the screening reached many thousands more.

Gently clowning with BBC styrofoam cups of water as they balanced precariously on his grand piano, Young performed solo on keyboard and acoustic guitar to a raptly attentive audience. He was feeling homesick for his ranch, he said, and couldn't wait to get back. He fumbled around endearingly for the right harmonica for each song that required one, confessing that he'd only recently taken the instrument seriously. In an unmemorable brown jacket and shoulder-length hair, he looked every inch the earnest singer-songwriter; it seemed hard to credit that this man was in fact one quarter of a rock'n'roll supergroup.

Yet if *Melody Maker*'s gossip column on 13 March was to believed, his stay in Britain had been cut short due to a bout of rock'n'roll-style behaviour. 'He flew back to America last week after being thrown out of his London flat . . . why? He was causing too much noise at five o'clock in the morning for three nights in succession,' it claimed.

On his return to the States, enforced or otherwise, Young had a back operation to ease his pain, and was advised to take exercise to keep the muscles developed in future. But if for nothing else, the year of '71 would be remembered for the May release of 'Four Way Street', a double-album resumé of Crosby, Stills, Nash & Young's stage work so far, which showed that the music that was going down was more than mildly memorable. Each of the discs separately showcased the acoustic and electric sides of CSN&Y's music.

The 'sideman' squabble having long since been resolved, Young was well represented, contributing three songs to the acoustic set in 'On The Way Home' (a nod to Springfield days), 'Cowgirl In The Sand' and 'Don't Let It Bring You Down'. The mainstays of the electric set were Young's 'Southern Man' and Stills' 'Carry On' at 13 and 14 minutes respectively; 'Ohio' was also represented, though in shorter form.

Melody Maker highlighted the extended tracks as 'electric music at its most self-indulgent. "Ohio" and "Long Time Gone" both come over well,' judged record reviewer Mark Plummer, 'but . . . the long blowing sessions could have been replaced by . . . more previously released material.'

Graham Nash evidently agreed, for when the album was reissued on compact disc in 1992, the extra space the format offered was used for the inclusion of four extra tracks. In strict keeping with the democracy of old, each protagonist was granted one apiece; Young struck luckiest, since his track was a ten-minute medley of three early favourites: 'The Loner', 'Cinnamon Girl' and 'Down By The River'.

'Four Way Street' soared to the top of the album chart in America, displacing Janis Joplin's 'Pearl' for a single week in May before giving way to the Rolling Stones' long-awaited 'Sticky Fingers'. In Britain, following his tour, Neil could look with satisfaction at 'Goldrush' at Number 7, with 'Four Way Street' at Number 5. In August, he began work on scoring music for his movie *Journey Through The Past*.

The year also saw him split from wife Susan and begin a relationship with actress Carrie Snodgress (whose initials CS would be found on every Young LP during their time together) Scott Young explained the marriage break-up thus: 'While Neil was away so much, Susan filled part of her time with her friends. The Topanga house he had wanted so much as a refuge was not that. For a brief time it had seemed not so important as the warmth and support of a marriage, but I heard from Neil later some kind of terse explanation: "It got so that every time I came home to Topanga, the house was full of people I didn't even know." That,' concluded his father, 'may be as much of an explanation as anyone is likely to get.'

Neil had called up Carrie to express his enjoyment of her performance in a recent film, *Diary Of A Mad Housewife*, for which she was nominated for an Oscar. They had agreed to meet, but when Young was confined to a hospital bed he called her up to cancel: but she came to the hospital anyway, and a relationship followed.

While still in that bed, Young gave an interview to journalist Ritchie Yorke, in which he sounded understandably road-weary. 'I've done three tours with Crazy Horse, two with the

bigger band (CSN&Y) and now I'm ready to just wrap it up. I want to bring it back to the roots again, do my gig and then I'm going to take a year off from touring.'

It had strongly been rumoured that the gap would be filled by a double live album, with tracks recorded at Carnegie Hall (New York), the Cellar Door (Washington) and, with Crazy Horse, the Fillmore East. This phantom LP would be the first of many never-released solo projects, following in the wake of the Springfield's legendary 'Stampede' – and, like that, would attain no little notoriety.

A spokesman had told *Melody Maker* that the album would be released in the States in March 1971: 'All that has to be completed is some of the mixing, which was delayed by his slipped disc.' The track listing included four Springfield songs ('I Am A Child', 'Expecting To Fly', 'Flying On The Ground' and 'Clancy'), three from 'Everybody Knows This Is Nowhere' (the title track, 'Down By The River', and 'Cowgirl In The Sand') and 'Ohio' from the CSN&Y repertoire.

Harvest

More interesting were a clutch of as yet unreleased songs. Some, like 'Old Man' and 'The Needle And The Damage Done', would appear on his next long-player, while 'Sugar Mountain' was the perennial B-side of 'Legend'. But some, like 'Bad Fog Of Loneliness' and 'Wondering' (a 'Goldrush' out-take) would never be released, while 'Dance Dance Dance' was given to Crazy Horse. Interestingly, too, 'See The Sky About To Rain' was slated for inclusion, though Young would not release this in studio form until 1974's 'On The Beach'.

In a career that has had many a peak and trough, Young's fourth solo album 'Harvest' remains his greatest success – certainly in commercial terms – over two decades from its March 1972 release.

If his first album encapsulated Young as singer-songwriter, the second Young the rocker and the third an amalgam of the two, then 'Harvest' swung back to the debut's introspective angle. And the timing could not have been better. Albums like Carole King's 'Tapestry' and James Taylor's 'Sweet Baby James' had sold in their millions and established a market for thoughtful, melodic material in an acoustic format. Indeed, Taylor and Linda Ronstadt both added their vocal harmonies to the album, having apparently been diverted from an intended appearance on a Johnny Cash television special! (Neil would later repay Ronstadt with 'Love Is A Rose', a song specially written for her.)

The midwife to that particular alliance was the Nashville producer Elliot Mazer, who had met Young by chance. He was asked to call members of Area Code 615, the supersession group made up of top Nashville pickers whose albums Mazer had overseen, and an immediate association was formed. 'I had no arrangement with Neil to work with him,' he explained later. 'We had met the night before and that was it. There was no contract, no legal situation.'

The Area Code musicians – Kenny Buttrey (drums), Troy Seals (bass) and Tony Joe White (guitar) – were summoned. 'Neil, when he plays a song, has a very specific beat and feel that he dictates by what he's playing,' Mazer continued. 'He offered a few suggestions to us as to the kinds of textures that he wanted, and some specific parts for the musicians. Neil's an editor: he'll say "Play less of this, less of that . . . " Those guys in Nashville were used to following singer-songwriters, it was astounding. We did those songs like "Old Man" and "Heart Of Gold" in a couple of hours, from the time Neil played the songs for the guys to the actual take with the back-up vocals on it. It was great magic.'

'Harvest' hit Number 1 in both America and the UK, with the single 'Heart Of Gold' reaching the top of the *Billboard* charts in mid-March. The song combined a mellow country-tinged sound with subtle lyrics that expressed a feeling that Young described as 'the frustrations of not being able to attain

what you want'. 'I was in and out of hospitals in the two years between "After The Goldrush" and "Harvest",' he told *Rolling Stone* three years later. 'I have one weak side and all the muscles slipped . . . I recorded most of "Harvest" in a brace. That's a lot of the reason it's such a mellow album. I couldn't physically play an electric guitar.'

The song's release as a single came about as something of a happy accident, he told the *Melody Maker* writer Ray Coleman. 'We went into the studio to cut the album, and I guess we were hot that night. It was a good cut, but it's gone now. I've seen a few artists who've got hung up on the singles market when they're really albums people. It's easy to do, but if you're wise you stay with being what you really are . . . I just hope there is not a single off my next album.'

Heavenly harmonies from the hottest act in the world – bar none – in the early Seventies. On CSN&Y's inevitable demise, groups like America were formed to fill the gap

His subsequent memories of 'Heart Of Gold' were somewhat tarnished, as the self-penned liner notes of the 'Decade' collection later explained in 1977. 'This song put me in the middle of the road. Travelling there soon became a bore so I headed for the ditch. A rougher ride, but I was meeting more interesting people there.'

It was to prove his most successful single ever. With the greatest of ironies, it was succeeded at the top by 'A Horse With No Name' by America, an all-singing acoustic three-piece who had prospered by filling the gap CSN&Y had left. The

song's writer Dewey Bunnell had an uncannily Young-like tone to his voice, employed to best effect on the 1972 smash which succeeded 'Heart Of Gold' at the top; few could have begrudged 'the real thing' his success after that.

Few, it seemed, but Bob Dylan, who said in *Spin* magazine some 13 years later that he'd considered the song a rip-off of his own sound. 'The only time it bothered me that someone sounded like me was when I was living in Phoenix, Arizona . . . the big song was "Heart Of Gold". I used to hate it when it came on the radio. I always liked Neil Young, but it bothered me every time I listened to "Heart Of Gold". I think it was up at Number 1 for a long time and I'd say "Shit, that's me. If it sounds like me, it should as well be me." It seemed to me that someone else had taken my thing and had run away with it. "

'Heart Of Gold' reached Number 10 in Britain. The follow-up, 'Old Man', also featuring Ronstadt and Taylor – was better received back home, where it peaked at Number 31 in June 1972. The song was inspired not by his father Scott Young as might be expected but by a ranch-hand called Louis who looked after Neil's livestock while he was on tour. The pair of orchestral-backed ballads, 'Words' and 'A Man Needs A Maid' (written about Carrie Snodgress) were, in retrospect, two of the least effective tracks.

Melody Maker's review of 'Harvest' in February 1972 suggested it held 'few surprises . . . the fairly familiar mixture of plangent rhythm guitar, woodchopping drums, stinging lead guitar and touches of steel, harmonica and piano.

'Melodically,' they noted, 'Young's songs have been getting gradually simpler, and some of the songs here, notably "Heart Of Gold" and "Are You Ready For The Country", are simple to the point of being facile . . . and yet he makes them work.'

This rare Norwegian picture sleeve for 'Heart Of Gold', Young's most successful ever single, makes the connection with the multi-platinum 'Harvest' album from which it was extracted

The album's British release was almost sabotaged by a pressing fault, revealed by *Melody Maker* in February 1972 under the headline 'Neil's Bitter Harvest'. An assistant at a major London record shop, Harlequin, reported that 95 per cent of the copies they'd sold had been returned because of surface noise – something the record company couldn't understand since 'Stampers were grown from the American mothers in order that we could match the American record exactly.' Fortunately, industrial action in the power industry had held up British production and a large number of imported American pressings had helped dilute the effects of any problem. Shades of the remixed first album . . . !

Matter of Honour

Crazy Horse, meanwhile, had maintained a solo career of their own – as much a matter of honour, one suspects, as anything else. Like 'The Rockets', this first album bore their name as a title and came out in February 1971. Reprise had picked them up in their own right, and appointed producers Jack Nitzsche and Bruce Botnick to steer them in the absence of their leader. Although no-one was to realise at the time, it would be the only Crazy Horse album to feature Danny Whitten, who shared six-string duties with Nils Lofgren.

And Lofgren it was who contributed the album's first highlight – 'Beggars Day', a song full of pent-up passion which would remain in his solo repertoire over the decades. Young donated 'Dance Dance Dance', a song he had earlier performed in concert but never recorded himself. Whitten's songs included 'I Don't Want To Talk About It' which would later become a middle-of-the-road pop standard in the hands of Rod Stewart. Other Whitten-penned highlights included 'Dirty, Dirty' (one of three tracks featuring Ry Cooder on lead guitar) and 'Downtown'; the latter would be picked up by British band Mott the Hoople, while Young himself would later resurrect it after its writer's death for 'Tonight's The Night'.

Self Indulgence

Melody Maker's Michael Watts dismissed 'Crazy Horse' in the first three words of his review. 'Neil Young revisited,' he sniffed. 'The main difference between Neil and his former backing group . . . is that he is good; they seldom rise above average.' Watts continued to make the parallel between 'Beggar's Day' and 'The Loner', 'Look At All The Things' and 'Country Girl' and even likened 'I Don't Want To Talk About It',

a song he conceded was 'one of the better tracks . . . a lovely song by any standards', to 'Only Love Can Break Your Heart Part Two'. Danny Whitten, Watts continued, 'does tend to phrase like you-know-who. Maybe, though, I am being too harsh on them.' All in all, though, 'I'd sooner have Crazy Horse with the chief in front.'

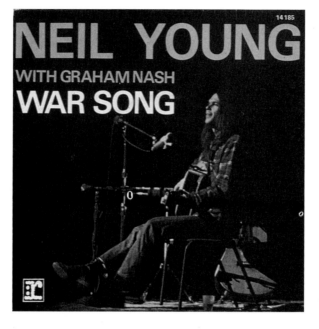

Sales matched reviews, and Crazy Horse's solo activities were put on hold. After Jack Nitzsche defected to rejoin Young in the Stray Gators and Lofgren

resumed his activities with Grin, they would enlist guitarist-vocalist Greg Leroy and, later, the Curtis Brothers, Michael and Rick. The latter would become successful songwriters, co-writing 'Southern Cross' with Steve Stills. Another of the songs they wrote, 'Blue Letter', would make them a steady income after being covered by Fleetwood Mac for their eponymous, multi-platinum-selling 1975 album.

So what had Neil Young been up to while Crazy Horse ran their own race? Musically speaking very little, if you discount a one-off union with Graham Nash entitled 'War Song'. Both a comment on the Vietnam war and the attempted assassination of Governor George Wallace, it stalled at the US Number 61

position in July. Another production, but one which had rather more far-reaching reverberations, was a first son, Zeke, born to Young and Carrie Snodgress on 8 September.

If 'Harvest' had represented a high water mark in sales terms, November brought the release of a double soundtrack LP which would prove a failure in both commercial and creative senses. Entitled 'Journey Through The Past', it consisted mainly of live recordings Young had made with Buffalo Springfield (from a television production called *The Hollywood Palace*), CSN&Y, Stray Gators and Crazy Horse, and would struggle to reached the Number 45 slot in the Billboard listings. The vaguely autobiographical film would premiere five months later in Dallas, but the album never received the critical acclaim of the order of either 'Harvest' or 'Goldrush'.

It's hardly difficult to see why Neil Young's many new-found fans, whether interested in his solo work or attracted via the previous CS&N connection, wouldn't take to the mish-mash soundtrack of a yet to be released film. Only one new song, 'Soldier', was featured, while the title track perversely was not. The release of the album had been stipulated by his record company as a payback for financing the movie, and it was they who'd delayed its release to a time when, with Christmas looming and a big-selling album fresh in everyone's minds, it could be expected to shift units.

But word soon got round. *Melody Maker*'s Alan Lewis was among the majority of reviewers who laid into Young without mercy, ensuring that the album would miss the British album chart entirely. 'Neil, was the journey really necessary?'

queried the headline over a picture captioned 'self-indulgent, frustrating, unworthy'. And that was just the sub-editors! 'Let the buyer beware,' intoned Lewis. 'This is not The New Neil Young Album in any meaningful sense . . . it's a ragbag collection . . . seemingly salvaged from the cutting-room floor, all stitched together with snatches of conversation, a bit of community singing, a few sound effects and a speech, courtesy of President Nixon.

'You could argue,' Lewis concluded, 'that this album is as mysterious, incomplete and explicit as the songs of the man himself. If so you may dig it. Personally I think it smacks of self-indulgence and laziness. Young has never been the most prolific writer, but a few new songs would have been worth far more than most of the overblown repetition contained here.'

The plot of the film seems to have centred around a character called the Graduate, who is beaten up and left for dead in a desert. His wanderings, in which the church and the US military both appear as threatening agencies, are interspersed with newsreel clips including footage of Nixon and the Ku Klux Klan. Viewed in retrospect, and particularly in the light of 'Rust Never Sleeps', the film version of *Journey* might well take on a new interest today, but it has yet to appear on video.

Young was unrepentant when facing *Rolling Stone* in 1975. 'I think it's a good film for a first film,' he insists, though admits, 'It's hard to say what the movie means.' His conclusion 'I made it for me . . . I never even had a script' added weight to the belief that this had in fact amounted to no more than self-indulgence of the highest order.

'Journey Through The Past' was clearly an unsatisfactory note on which to end the first solo chapter of the Neil Young story. To an innocent observer, the choice for the future seemed simple: cut out the blind alleys and progress creatively and commercially, either solo or as part of Crosby, Stills, Nash and Young. With Neil Young, though, life would never be quite that simple . . .

Opposite: 'War Song', a very rare single collaboration with Graham Nash, sold poorly on its summer 1972 release

Above: More bedsit balladeering from Neil

Neil Young (1969)

Released a little too soon to benefit from the imminent singer-songwriter boom of the early Seventies that made artists like Carole King household names, 'Neil Young' was less than an earth-shattering release; only 'The Loner' would make it onto an all-time 'Best Of' collection, and that was in a substantialy shorter, tighter form than the concert epic it would eventually become. In many ways, the album closed a first chapter rather then heralding a career, since Neil Young's future recordings would be generally less nostalgic and introspective .

'Neil Young' is available in both its original and remixed form; all CD issues of the album boast the remix, and also carry the lyrics and illustrations from the original American gatefold sleeve which were never seen on the British version at the time.

Track Listing:

The Emperor Of Wyoming • The Loner • If I Could Have Her Tonight • I've Been Waiting For You • The Old Laughing Lady • String Quartet From Whiskey Boot Hill • Here We Are In The Years • What Did You Do To My Life • I've Loved Her So Long • The Last Trip To Tulsa

Retrospective (1969)

The timing of this album was unfortunate, coming slap bang in the middle of Young's rapid-fire first solo releases, but effectively encapsulated Buffalo Springfield's finest moments. Indeed, it equalled their highest US album chart placing by peaking at Number 42, bringing Atlantic/Atco an immediate return on their earlier investment.

Six of the 12 songs were Young compositions, reflecting his perceived solo status rather than indicating a dominance of his former group's music, and were the obvious choices: one from the first, three from the second and two from the third albums.

An eponymous double album compilation was released four years later, but 'Retrospective' remains the first, most successful and most readily available summation of Buffalo Springfield's brief, bright, two-year recording history.

Track Listing:

For What It's Worth • Mr Soul • Sit Down I Think I Love You • Kind Woman • Bluebird • On The Way Home • Nowadays Clancy Can't Even Sing • Broken Arrow • Rock'n'Roll Woman • I Am A Child • Go And Say Goodbye • Expecting To Fly

Everybody Knows
This Is Nowhere (1969)

The first recorded union of Young and Crazy Horse, this album reached Number 24 in America and laid down many of Young's future trademarks. 'Down By The River and 'Cowgirl In The Sand' were simple, three-chord romps dominated by the kind of extended soloing CSN&Y's rigid song structures rarely permitted. His sound was harsh and uncompromising, guitar partner Danny Whitten providing a sympathetic foil.

'Cinnamon Girl', Young's first US hit single, compressed the album's dynamic appeal into three minutes, while there were contrasting acoustic interludes in 'Round And Round' and 'Running Dry'. But the album's abiding impression was of liberation from commercial considerations, something his work with Crazy Horse (prominently and unselfishly billed on the sleeve) would all too often demonstrate.

Track Listing:

Cinnamon Girl • Everybody Knows This Is Nowhere • Round And Round • Down By The River • The Losing End • Running Dry (Requiem For The Rockets) • Cowgirl In The Sand

Déjà Vu (1970)

'Déjà Vu' was Young's only studio album with Crosby, Stills & Nash prior to 1988's 'American Dream' and, although released nearly halfway through 1970, became the year's best-selling American album. It had reportedly taken 800 man hours to record and included three US hit singles in 'Woodstock', 'Our House' and 'Teach Your Children'. Young contributed two tracks, 'Helpless' and 'Country Girl', also co-writing the closing 'Everybody I Love You' with Stills. The quartet was augmented in the studio by drummer, Dallas Taylor and bassist Greg Reeves, who also appeared on the sleeve alongside the principals.

'Déjà Vu' took us into the Seventies with a genuine feeling of warmth and optimism: its bookend was perhaps the Eagles' bleak 'Hotel California', which as early as 1976 was exposing the whole American West Coast dream as being something of a sham.

Track Listing:

Carry On • Teach Your Children • Almost Cut My Hair • Helpless • Woodstock • Déjà Vu • Our House • 4+20 • Country Girl • Everybody I Love You

After The Goldrush (1970)

Encompassing ecology (the title track), politics ('Southern Man') and love songs, 'After The'Goldrush' was Young's first album to go Top Ten in the States, its initial success undoubtedly due to the exposure CSN&Y had brought. Musically, it combined the naive singer-songwriting of his first album with Crazy Horse-style rockers like 'Southern Man' and 'When You Dance I Can Really Love' plus a rare cover version, Don Gibson's 'Oh Lonesome Me'.

Having aborted original recording sessions with Crazy Horse, his main featured musician was Nils Lofgren, the young leader of Washington band Grin, on guitar, piano and harmony vocals. Despite a shifting cast that included Stills, Greg Reeves, Crazy Horse (eventually) and Jack Nitzsche, 'Goldrush' took little more than a fortnight to record at Young's Topanga home.

Track listing:
Tell Me Why • After The Goldrush • Only Love Can Break A Heart • Southern Man • Till The Morning Comes • Oh Lonesome Me • Don't Let It Bring You Down • Birds • When You Dance I Can Really Love You • I Believe In You • Cripple Creek Ferry

Four Way Street
(with Crosby, Stills & Nash) (1971)

Nash and Stills were the prime movers in this live momento of the short-lived supergroup, though engineer Bill Halverson had to play mediator. 'I think I finished that album twenty times before they all said, "Okay, put it out"', he recalled. Despite the deliberate lack of overdubs, it remains a worthy souvenir of the moment that none of the participants need be ashamed of and deserved its US Number 1 status.

The later double CD reissue included a three-song Neil Young medley that had previously remained unheard for space reasons.

Track listing:
Suite: Judy Blue Eyes • On The Way Home • Teach Your Children • Triad • The Lee Shore • Chicago • Right Between The Eyes • Cowgirl In The Sand • Don't Let It Bring You Down • 49 Bye Byes/America's Children • Love The One You're With • Pre Road Downs • Long Time Gone • Southern Man • Ohio • Carry On • Find The Coast Of Freedom • (Reissue bonus tracks) King Midas In Reverse • Laughing • Black Queen • Medley: The Loner • Cinnamon Girl • Down By The River

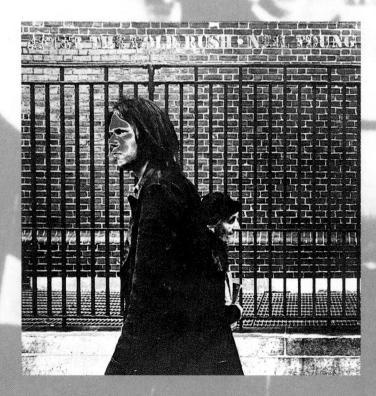

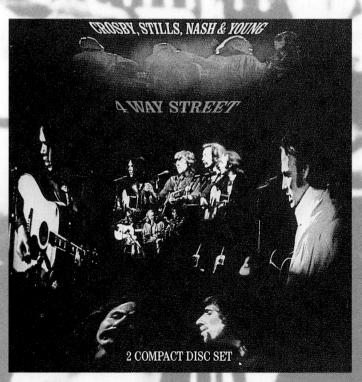

Harvest (1972)

Patched together from various sessions over a period of a year, 'Harvest' reaped the rewards that Neil Young's earlier work had so richly deserved.

The unstoppable impetus of two genuine hit singles, 'Heart Of Gold' and 'Old Man', made it a transatlantic chart topper, while the sugar-coated melody of 'The Needle And The Damage Done' barely concealed what was just the first of many anti-drug lyrics, recorded live after Danny Whitten's death from an overdose.

The ornate arrangements – with the London Symphony Orchestra – of 'There's A World' and 'A Man Needs A Maid' brought the Jack Nitzsche era to an end, and indeed while 'Harvest' could well have represented the first of a string of platinum solo albums, it actually marked the commercial peak that Young would spend the rest of the decade striving to escape from.

Track Listing:

Out On The Weekend • Harvest • Man Needs A Maid • Heart Of Gold • Are You Ready For The Country? • Old Man • There's A World • Alabama • The Needle And The Damage Done • Words (Between The Lines Of Age)

Journey Through The Past (Soundtrack) (1972)

Held back at record company request, 'Journey Through The Past' successfully dissipated all the commercial momentum 'Harvest' had accrued; indeed, it's arguable that only Lou Reed, with 'Metal Machine Music', has managed to top it in terms of commercial suicide.

Had this mix of sacred songs, a Beach Boys instrumental and live material from Springfield, CSN&Y and Crazy Horse been sold as a low-price bootleg it might have been better received; instead, it came in a die-cut, foldout sleeve with picture bags. Only a version of 'Ohio' that bettered its 'Four Way Street' counterpart and a new song, 'Soldier', made this bizarre release worthwhile for the Young completist.

Track listing:

For What It's Worth/Mr Soul • Rock'n'Roll Woman • Find The Cost Of Freedom • Ohio • Southern Man • Are You ready For The Country • Let Me Call You Sweetheart • Alabama • Words (Between The Lines Of Age) • Relativity Invitation • Handel's Messiah • King Of Kings • Soldier • Let's Go Away For Awhile

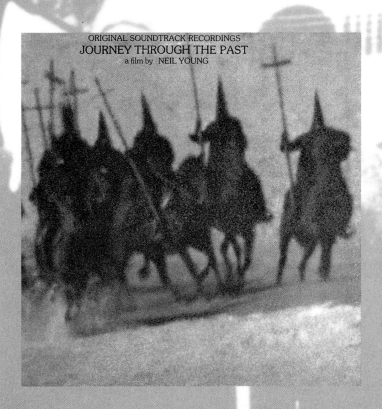

1973 – 1979

Diamonds & Rust

'For the first time in my life, I couldn't get anything to turn out the way I wanted it,' Young would later complain of the next phase of his career which was to lead him on a journey to hell and back.

And yet for the man seemingly with music's Midas touch, 1973 should have opened on a high with the original Byrds (old 'rivals' from Springfield days) covering not one but two of his songs for their eponymous reunion album for Asylum Records, 'Cowgirl In The Sand' and the yet-to-be-released 'See The Sky About To Rain'.

But the new year had already been tainted by the sudden death of Crazy Horse guitarist and close friend Danny Whitten from a drug overdose on 18 November 1972, a tragedy that was to have far-reaching repercussions on Young and his music for years to come.

His immediate reaction to his friend's death was to immerse himself in roadwork; 1973 saw him out on the road again, setting off in January on a marathon three-month, 65-city US tour with ad-hoc band the Stray Gators – drummer Kenny Buttrey (soon to be replaced by John Barbata), bassist Tim Drummond, pedal steel player Ben Keith and the ubiquitous Jack Nitzsche on keyboards.

Whitten had originally been brought in as lead guitarist but was still trying to kick his habit, and it only took one rehearsal at Neil's ranch to prove he was still in poor shape. He was sent back to LA with a plane ticket and $50 in his pocket, which on arrival back home he apparently used to score the pure heroin that killed him.

While darkness and despair covered Neil Young's world, America's box-office managers were certainly doing well from the tour. March brought a sold-out date at New York's prestigious Carnegie Hall, but the tour was certainly not a happy one. There were major problems with both the band and the road crew who were demanding more dollars and a split of the profits. And when Young's voice began to falter, he sent an SOS to his old pals, Crosby and Nash, whose harmony vocals and moral support helped him get through the last 19 dates. But playing to mammoth 20,000-seater auditoria was far from a

Young goes electric as his early-Seventies dream goes sour and the high hopes of 'Harvest' give way to grim reality. He cut an increasingly harrowing figure on stage as the decade wore on

Above: The earlier harmony achieved with Crosby, Stills and Nash proved impossible to regain despite several abortive attempts in the Seventies

Opposite: Hair flying and resplendent in patched workshirt, the Neil Young of the Seventies became ever more angst-ridden, turning out high-energy electric rock

satisfying experience, as Young went on to tell *Melody Maker*'s editor-in-chief Ray Coleman:

'I want to be able to see the people I'm playing for and I want the people to feel that the music is being made just for them – you bounce off people that way, get up, jump around, have a good time, get drunk – I've been right through that trip of massive audiences and my ego has been satisfied. I guess I had to do it, but once you've done it, then what? You realise that is not what communicating is all about.'

His film *Journey Through The Past* premiered on 8 April at the Dallas Film Festival where its two showings drew the biggest crowds of the week. When his name appeared on screen the applause was immediate and sustained, but rather more reserved after the film finished. Young, who had been watching from the projection booth, then walked to the front, sitting on the lip of the stage to answer audience questions for half an hour. He explained that the film had cost about $350,000 and had grown from playing around with a new movie camera in Topanga.

Fantasy and Fiction

Producer Fred Underhill was perhaps more revealing. In a later interview, he said, 'It's a conscious attempt not to do a music film, a performance film. He ventured into fantasy and did fictional sequences. But it also has his music and some historical context for it, from TV films of Buffalo Springfield through today.' Even he, though, had to admit, 'I keep asking Neil what it's about, too.'

When Warners withdrew their distribution for the film, a proposed CSN&Y reunion seemed a very attractive notion, especially with rehearsals at the resort of Lahaina on the Hawaiian island of Maui. The intention was to record an album with the tentative title of 'Human Highway' (named after a Young original). A cover photo of the four tanned protagonists, shot at sunset on the island on the last day of their stay, eventually wound up as part of the packaging for 1991's 'Crosby, Stills & Nash' boxed-set retrospective.

Inevitably all the old rivalry began to scupper the project, and despite the quartet later reconvening at Young's ranch the whole project was aborted. A number of strong new songs made it to tape before the plug was pulled; these included the title track, two Nash compositions 'And So it Goes' and 'Prison Song', plus Young's 'Sailboat Song' which would later appear under the guise of 'Through My Sails' on Neil's 'Zuma' set. But it all came to nothing when the petty squabbling began again and when no consensus could be reached as to whether the band should tour or finish the album first.

On returning to LA from Hawaii Neil had been greeted with the grim news that another good friend, CSN&Y guitar-tuner

Bruce Berry, had met a similar fate to Danny Whitten. This, it seemed, was the straw that broke the camel's back – and in an attempt to ease the pain, not for the first time, he buried himself in a new project and gathered up the remnants of Crazy Horse. Retreating to the small Rehearsal Hall D of Studio Instrumentals in Hollywood, Molina, Talbot and Young were joined by Nils Lofgren and Ben Keith.

Talking later of these sessions Young remembered:

'I'm not a junkie, and I won't even try it out to check what it's like. But we'd get really high – drink a lot of tequila, get right out on the edge, where we knew we were so screwed up that we could easily just fall on our faces, and not be able to handle it as musicians. We'd wait until the middle of the night, wait until the vibe hit and then we'd do it.'

Bass player Billy Talbot has similar if not so painful memories: 'It was an art project. We'd go in every day to SIR (Studio Instrument Rentals). There was a wooden stage, a mobile truck in the back and the producer would be in the back with us. We'd do the whole album in a row, like, it meant something. Then we'd take a break and do it all again later on in the night, a little drunker. It was as pure as we could get it.'

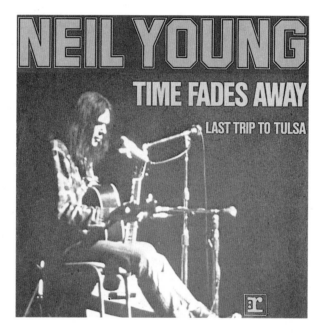

Welcome to Miami Beach
The result was 'Tonight's The Night', probably Young's most harrowing album to date. Producer David Briggs was back in the fold after two years out of the picture. (He'd been running a recording studio near Toronto, but when the businessman backing it sunk money into an ill-fated pop festival the studio ended up a casualty. Briggs decided to return to California and Young's side.)

It was a fraught period in which to return, as Briggs later recalled. 'One day in the summer of 1973 there was a knock on my door. I opened it and there was Neil. He said, "Hey, I was just on my way to a CSN&Y session, and I just don't feel like going there. Let's go make some rock'n'roll." So we packed our bags and came down to LA, and wound up with the "Tonight's The Night" album.' But before its release could even be considered, the band went out on the road.

Young and Crazy Horse opened LA's Roxy Theatre on 20 September 1973 with the first of eight shows on four nights with Graham Nash as opening act. As the tour hit Europe, audiences expecting the soft rock of yore were dumbfounded by the sight of Young as a sleazy Master of Ceremonies, the stage adorned with old bits of junk, palm trees, even a wooden Indian and a bright red neon sign proclaiming 'Welcome To Miami Beach', a solitary naked light bulb casting a sickly glow over the whole proceedings. The music was rough and ready, with most of it unfamiliar and uncompromising. Halfway through the show, Young would announce to the audience: 'Welcome to Miami Beach, ladies and gentlemen. Everything is cheaper than it looks. All of my grandmothers and grandfathers come from Miami Beach!'

There would be no let-up as fans were relentlessly treated to one new song after another – 'Tonight's The Night', 'Albuquerque', 'New Mama', 'Speakin' Out' – all performed in a ramshackle and discordant way. Only the show's finale offered any relief when a few old favourites such as 'Cinammon Girl', 'Helpless' and 'Southern Man' were dusted down. Just to rub a little salt into his fans' wounds, the support slot featured the tuneful, clean and countrified rock of the Eagles, then beginning their own dizzying ascent to stardom with the 'Desperado' album. As the tour progressed, a new record appeared, 'Time Fades Away' – which, in its own way, was just as perplexing as the music going down in the live venues.

Opposite: French release of 'Time Fades Away', a single from the live album of the same name, cut in 1973 accompanied by the Stray Gators and featuring all new material

Above: Rocking later in the decade with Crazy Horse

'Time', his first 'live' album and a document of the earlier, ill-starred Stray Gators tour, was a nerve-wracking work of entirely new material. Looking at it retrospectively in *Melody Maker*, Allan Jones described it as 'the first act in a three-part series of albums which amount to a complete reassessment of (Young's) place in the scheme of things . . . is possibly (his) masterpiece . . . it's raw and passionate, an anguished scream of rejection, full-blooded and overflowing with manic energy; we're projected straight on to Pain Street with the junkies and the damned in a desperate and fearsome collision of sound.'

'Don't Be Denied', the confident opening shot, was one of the record's highlights, a thumbnail autobiographical sketch weighing the material gains of superstardom against fears for his own spiritual decline. Despite catching the Christmas sales tide, the sales figures reflected that Neil's new direction wasn't to everyone's taste and peaked at Number 22 in the US and Number 20 in the UK. A 'competitor' in the racks at the time was a double compilation of Buffalo Springfield material that reached US Number 104 in the wake of the success achieved by Stills, Young, Furay and Messina in their respective post-Springfield projects.

Young's own view of 'Time Fades Away' is revealing. 'It makes you feel uneasy to listen to it,' he told his father Scott

for his book *Neil And Me*. 'The only redeeming factor was that it truly reflected where I was at. It was a chapter that I wish hadn't been written but I knew I had to get it out because I knew it represented something . . . Some people have come up to me and said "I love that record" . . . but not many.'

'Tonight's The Night' encountered just as low-key a reception when his record company refused to release it, considering it commercial suicide for the one-time 'Harvest' hitmaker. Young recalled this incident when talking to Adam Sweeting in *Melody Maker* 12 years later. 'I would describe that as a rocky day. They couldn't believe how rough and sloppy it was, they couldn't believe that I really wanted to put it out. I said, "That's it, that's the way it's going out."'

Broken Dreams

An impasse was reached, and an unrepentant Young re-entered the studio with a different crew – one that even impressed Reprise. Crosby and Nash, Band members Rick Danko and Levon Helm, regular Young sidemen Keith, Talbot and Ralph Molina and fiddle player Rusty Kershaw were all involved in the sessions for 'On The Beach', an album released in June 1974. Compared with 'Tonight's The Night', this new work was more resigned, with some distance now between Young and the traumas of the months before.

Even so, it was hardly easy listening, as the album sleeve (depicting a missile buried in the sand) confirmed. It saw Young cogitating not only on personal feelings stemming from the deaths of his friends, but on wider issues such as the broken dreams of the Sixties.

This theme was brought home on one of the key cuts, 'Revolution Blues', wherein Neil assumed the persona of Charles Manson, the murderer who brought the optimism of the previous decade to a sickening conclusion with the deaths of Sharon Tate and other Laurel Canyon celebrities. It found Young in the guise of the homicidal maniac living in a trailer on the edge of town 'with 25 rifles just to keep the population down . . . I'm a barrel of laughs with my carbine on, I keep 'em hoppin' till my ammunition's gone.'

In reality, Neil had met Manson at (Beach Boy) Dennis Wilson's house as he recalled years later in *Melody Maker*:

'He was a very intense individual. He was looking to get a recording contract and I actually told Mo Ostin at Warners about him! I did also warn him that Charlie was a little . . . uh . . . well, like I say, intense . . . he never sang the same song twice. He made the songs up as he went along. Each song was a new one, every time he sang . . . I was fascinated by him. By his force. His creative force . . . it was kind of an uneasy feeling, being around Charlie, yeah. He'd been in jail a lot. And I attributed his strangeness partly to the fact that I thought he wasn't used to being out on the street.'

Asked in the same interview whether he saw a reflection of his own personality in Manson's, he chortled:

'No, I'm pretty straight myself . . . Well, I guess I do have a violent side . . . I hope it's more under control nowadays. But, yeah, I'm an extremist. I guess I'd have to own up to that one.'

'On The Beach' ended with the extended, pained 'Ambulance Blues', where Young pondered the emptiness brought by stardom and personal tragedy, accompanied by acoustic guitar and violin, and tries to face up to it. It climaxes with the immortal lines, 'You're all just pissin' in the wind, you don't know it but you are' (attributed to manager Elliot Roberts). On one level it represented a broadside at his pals Crosby Stills and Nash, on another, that all the hopes and aspirations of the hippy generation were ultimately doomed.

Despite its defiant air of honesty and despite the strong cast list, 'On The Beach' met with mixed reviews. It charted at Number 16 in the US and 42 in the UK, while the single 'Walk On' reached a mere Number 69 in the US. *Melody Maker* called it 'nemesis rock . . . a depressing album', even accusing it of 'talent squandered'. Young later admitted:

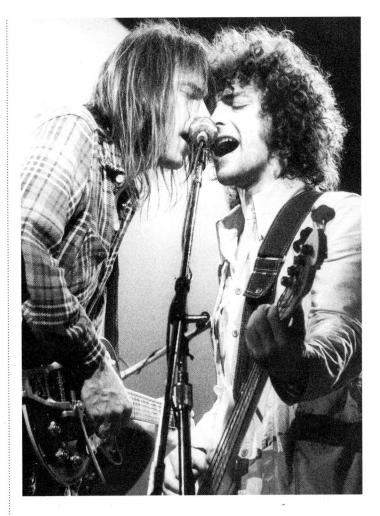

Above: Bass player Billy Talbot was to prove a constant and loyal companion to Neil Young in his journey through the Seventies, along with his Crazy Horse compadré, drummer Ralph Molina

Opposite: The manic Young of 'Tonight's The Night' infamy. The deaths of Bruce Berry and Danny Whitten caused much soul-searching and inspired some moving music

'I was pretty down I guess at the time, but I just did what I wanted to do . . . I think if everybody looks back at their own lives they'll realise that they all went through something like that. There are periods of depression, periods of elation, of optimism and scepticism, the whole thing . . . it just keeps coming in waves. You go down to the beach and watch the same thing, just imagine every wave is a different set of emotions coming in. Just keep coming. As long as you don't ignore it, it'll still be there.

'If you start shutting yourself off and just not letting yourself live through the things that are coming through you, I think that's when people start getting older really fast, and that's when they really age. Cos they decide that they're happy to be what they were at a certain time in their lives when they were happiest, and they say, "That's where I'm gonna be for the rest of of my life." And from that moment on they're dead, y'know, just walking around to avoid that.'

Rather than go out and promote 'On The Beach' alone, Young did a complete about-turn and agreed to another CSN&Y reunion – a huge stadium tour, and in view of his previous comments deriding large venues, the venture met with accusations that they were doing it purely for the money. After the event, Young told *Rolling Stone*:

'There's no question that we got paid a lot of money for doing it. But there's no question that we were all there and delivered every night.'

The tour, which climaxed at London's Wembley Stadium on 14 September in front of 72,000 people, also starred Joni

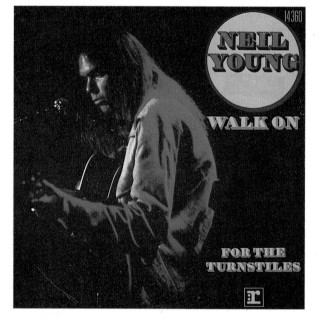

Mitchell, the Band and Jesse Colin Young and reputedly grossed $11 million. Steve Stills, discussing the tour in *CS&N: The Authorised Biography*, was less guarded than Young about his motivation for the reunion:

'I'd gotten married, my son Christopher was being born and my financial situation was starting to get a little strange.'

Whatever the reasons, relations between the four superstars were sunny, and during the course of the tour, later dubbed 'the first real stadium tour' by impresario Bill Graham, the quartet – backed up by Tim Drummond on bass, Joe Lala on percussion and Russ Kunkel on drums – did indeed 'deliver every night'. Kicking off the dates in Seattle on 9 July, the band were on immediate form – no one could have guessed that this show in the Pacific Northwest was in reality a warm-up.

Their first appearance, spread over three-and-a-half hours, was all it took to re-establish CSN&Y as the quintessential harmony-rockers bar none. The quartet proved right from the start that it wasn't about to hand its crown over to any other pretender, be they America, Loggins & Messina, the Eagles or any other outfit who'd risen to prominence during their four-year absence.

Young played host to rehearsals for the tour at his idyllic Broken Arrow ranch in the Santa Cruz Mountains. Rehearsing outside on a huge, custom-built Redwood stage, the band

Above: 'Walk On', the single taken from 'On The Beach', was as commercially unsuccessful as its parent album.

Right: Letting loose on stage

relearned their parts and in Neil's studio even cut some more tracks such as the still-to-be-issued 'Little Blind Fish'. During the tour, however, Young maintained a discreet distance from his colleagues, choosing to avoid off-stage contact by travelling from gig to gig in his GMC camper van with son Zeke, his dog Art and two friends his only companions.

Among the 40-plus songs included in their live repertoire was 'On The Beach's 'Revolution Blues', the presence of which caused no little discomfiture to other band members.

'David Crosby especially was very uncomfortable,' Neil later recalled, 'because it was so much the darker side. They all wanted to put out the light, y'know, make people feel good and happy and everything, and that song was like a wart or something on the perfect beast.'

After the high of the London show, Neil took off in his recently acquired 1934 Rolls Royce (which, in a fit of characteristic whimsy, he'd christened 'Wembley'!) on a tour of Wales and Scotland, then cut short a proposed trip to Amsterdam with Nash to head off home. Not all band members recalled this tour with fondness: Crosby, who nicknamed it 'The Doom Tour', was highly critical.

'I didn't dig playin' stadiums,' he groused later. 'That was Neil and Stephen's trip, especially Stephen's. He was into being bigger than the Stones. Bigger than everybody. But the music suffered, I feel. When we got into the electric set, Neil and Stephen started competing on guitar simply by turning up. We clocked 'em once and they got up to 135 decibels. So Nash and I were unable to sing harmony. It was a drag.'

Yet Crosby put aside such negative feelings as work recommenced on the CSN&Y album they'd begun to woodshed at the Broken Arrow ranch. It was a record of which Crosby would later eulogise. 'It would have been the best one, man,' he insisted. 'You should have heard us. "Wind On The Water", "Human Highway" . . . we cut "Homeward Through The Haze" . . . Stephen and Neil playing guitar, Nash on organ, me on piano, Russ Kunkel on drums, Leland Sklar on bass. We smoked and burned!'

Profoundly Passionate

Differences of opinion set in during sessions at the Record Plant in Sausalito, and Young at length packed his bags and disappeared to begin the groundwork for a new solo record in LA. A typically forthright Graham Nash saw this as yet another cynical betrayal on Young's part: 'Neil utilised CS&N as a springboard for his own career. It was a very deliberate move and well done. As soon as CS&N didn't suit him, he sloughed us off like an old snakeskin.'

Even without Neil Young, his colleagues could make little or no headway. 'There was doom in the room', recalls Nash, arguments breaking out between him and Stephen Stills over a harmony part which resulted in Stills violently attacking the master tape of 'Wind On The Water' with a razorblade! By the beginning of 1975, the much awaited reunion album was as dead as a dodo.

Ironically, 'Homegrown', the album Young had quit to begin, would never see the official light of day either. It was reputed to be a return to the style of albums like 'After The Goldrush', the perfect tonic for the legions of fans upset by the downer mood of its predecessors. The mainly acoustic album, which was recorded in Nashville with Elliot Mazer once again at the production helm, featured Tim Drummond on bass, Rufus Thibodeaux on violin, Ben Keith on steel guitar, Karl Himmel on drums, and with harmonies supplied by Emmylou Harris.

When the finished project was played back at a private party, the new tunes apparently failed to have the desired effect on Young's invited audience. As luck would have it, someone then put on the other side of the tape which con-

Opposite: Neil in concert in September 1974, the rocking chair and jeans harking back to a mythical America that perhaps only ever existed in the minds of romantic poets, film makers, painters and songwriters

Above: On stage once again with old buddies Crosby Stills and Nash in 1974

Above: Neil made just one trip to Great Britain in 1971, when he appeared at the prestigious Royal Festival Hall on London's South Bank

Opposite: Likewise, paying yet another brief visit to the United Kingdom – here he is in action in London in 1976, at the Hammersmith Odeon

tained the revamped 'Tonight's The Night' (resequenced, at Elliot Roberts' suggestion, for a potential Broadway show based on the life of Bruce Berry), at which everyone visibly brightened; Rick Danko immediately insisted that Neil release it instead of 'Homegrown'.

Quite how Young persuaded the execs at Reprise to give 'Tonight' the green light the second time around has never been revealed (Scott Young surmises that they had heard material from his relatively commercial next album, 'Zuma', and thought they could release it hard on the heels of this one). Whatever the truth, it was to herald Neil's mid-Seventies 'renaissance' – if not in immediate sales terms, then certainly among the critics baying for his blood.

'Tonight's The Night' finally appeared 23 months after its first version had been recorded. *Melody Maker* commented: 'It represents Young at his most emotionally committed and gives us a fascinating view of his fierce determination to break free of the artistic strait-jacket which had been constraining him since before "Harvest".'

It was rare for rival organ *New Musical Express* to agree, but an ecstatic Nick Kent pronounced it 'one of the most profoundly passionate, important rock albums ever made.'

The album as a whole took no prisoners, songs like the eponymous title cut oozing with the raw sensitivity of an open wound. 'I wasn't even sure then that I even wanted it to come out,' Young would confide years later. 'It was like a wake, an Irish wake. We did it for Danny and Bruce Berry and those guys, all the others like 'em that never came through.'

The version that eventually reached the record stores was a somewhat toned-down affair, as Young would later attest in *Melody Maker*:

'The original version of "Tonight's The Night" was somewhat heavier than the one that hit the stands. The original one had only nine songs on it. They were the same takes, but the songs that were missing were "Lookout Joe" and "Borrowed Tune", a couple of songs that I added. They both fitted lyrically but they softened the blow of the album a little bit.

'What happened was the original had only nine songs but it had a lot of talking, a lot of mumbling and talking between the group and me, more disorganised and fucked-up sounding than the songs, but they were intros to the songs. Not counts but little discussions, three-and four-word conversations between songs, and it left it with a very spooky feeling. It was like you didn't know if these guys were still gonna be alive in the morning . . . it was really too strong.

'I never even played it for the record company like that. We made our own decision not to do that. If they thought "Tonight's The Night" was too much the way it came out which they did, a lot of people – they're lucky they didn't hear the other one.'

The released version would sell many more copies in the 1980s that it did when it first appeared; indeed, Young told his father Scott that Reprise 'printed the bare minimum and tried to take it off the re-order lists. You couldn't even get it. We got on the case, and when it came time to renegotiate, one thing put into my contract was that everything I make stays in print – whether it's selling or not.'

Love at First Sight

Meanwhile, Young had fallen back in with his old partners Crazy Horse. In early 1975 Billy Talbot contacted Neil with the promising news that he'd been working with a new guitarist who he thought might just fit the bill as a replacement for Danny Whitten – one Frank 'Poncho' Sampedro. Since their self-titled debut album, Crazy Horse had become a separate entity pursuing what could only be described as a somewhat erratic career of their own, recording two patchy works on the Epic label, 'Loose' and 'At Crooked Lake', both of which sorely lacked Whitten's rare talents as a lead guitar player, singer and songwriter.

They'd hit something of a hiatus in the summer of 1973 when Young recalled Talbot and Molina for the bemusing 'Tonight's The Night' tour. In its aftermath at a party in LA, Talbot chanced upon Sampedro who had played guitar in high-school boogie bands back in Detroit. After an excursion to Mexico the pair returned home, linked up with Molina and began writing songs and playing together.

Ralph and Billy's commitments to the 'On The Beach' sessions meant that the 'new' Crazy Horse could only begin serious practising in early 1975, working up some fine new tunes that would take a further three years before being vinylised! The trio was fired up and hot to trot, as Molina recalled in *BAM* magazine:

'It got real natural. When we played, the music started to flow just like we wanted it to. So it was real easy to start coming out, working on our own songs.'

Having just recovered the Les Paul guitar whose scorching tone had given 'Everybody Knows This Is Nowhere' such a distinctive edge, Young headed over to Talbot's home in Echo Park to meet Whitten's heir apparent. It was love at first sight, Young picking up on what Sampedro had called the 'magical energy' and brokering the deal: 'I'll help you do these songs if you'll do this record'. The quartet relocated to producer David Briggs's house at Zuma beach and got down to business.

Return from the Twilight Zone

Released in November 1975, 'Zuma' reflected Young's new-found positivism, overflowing with upbeat tunes driven by ferocious riffs and buoyed by his rediscovered ear for melody. The maestro had returned from the twilight zone! Although many of the songs still dealt with the themes of lost love and its effects, their author was no longer drowning himself in a sea of self-pity.

Backed by Crazy Horse on six out of the nine cuts, Young bristled with energy and freshness. 'Don't Cry No Tears', the opener, hints back at the commercial potential of earlier times with an infectious refrain on the chorus; interestingly, given its youthful exuberance, it had been reworked from an original song written back in his Canadian youth. The single 'Lookin' For A Love' was almost as catchy, though it failed to set the charts on fire in the same way 'Heart Of Gold' had done. 'Barstool Blues' was more autobiographical (during the sessions Sampedro had introduced Neil to the pleasures of American bar culture!), while 'Cortez The Killer' was the album's magnificent centrepiece, Young weaving the tale of the bloodthirsty Spanish conquistador plundering the Inca kingdom with a more personalised love story.

'Cortez' is a classic, perfectly highlighting, on a slow hallucinatory seven-minute voyage, the shimmering twin-guitar play of Crazy Horse, that had made 'Down By The River' and 'Cowgirl In The Sand' such exciting and intrinsic staples of Young's repertoire. It was adventurous, reconfirming that Young had lost none of his ability to experiment away from shorter song structures.

The album played calmly out on 'Through My Sails', effectively a 'wooden' CSN&Y track with Young on acoustic, Stills on bass and Russ Kunkel on congas. After the feisty 'Cortez', it was a fitting note on which to end, with Crosby's vocals particularly shining through. Of this work, Young would later attest: '"Zuma" was breaking free of the murk. My best albums are the ones with Crazy Horse. They're the most fluid. "Zuma" was a great electric album coming from a place where pop leaves rock'n'roll.' The public agreed, hoisting the album to Number 44 in Britain and Number 25 Stateside.

From a commercial standpoint, Young was once again getting back on track. Yet if a return to stadium status beckoned, his next move was, predictably perhaps, the exact opposite.

Inspired by Dylan's 'Rolling Thunder Revue' that was taking the East Coast by storm that winter, Young set off on some low-key Californian dates in December that became known as

the 'Rolling Zuma Revue'! (He'd recovered quickly from a successful throat operation in October.)

With Crazy Horse backing him up, Young played small bars such as the Cotati and the Marshall tavern. In some places there were as little as 50 people in the audience and at others there wasn't even an admission charge. He would sometimes take a back seat during the set, thereby allowing Crazy Horse to perform some of their own songs like 'Lost And Lonely' and 'I'm Just A Man'. And, of course, in addition to the crowd favourites such as 'Southern Man' and 'Don't Cry No Tears', Young would feel the need to slip in a host of more unfamiliar titles such as 'Spud Blues (Country Home)', 'Homegrown' and 'Like A Hurricane'.

The bar shows carried over into January, allowing the quartet to hone down their material for a large overseas tour of Japan and Europe, which met with great audience and critical acclaim, successfully repairing the foundations of Young's reputation so badly damaged by the autumn 1973 gigs. Allan Jones was so impressed by their Hammersmith Odeon shows of 29 and 30 March, he wrote in *Melody Maker*: 'It's extremely unlikely that we shall witness a performance more impressive from an artist of such stature again this year.'

Such enthusiasm matched the feelings within the band, as Billy Talbot was later to recall: 'We started to really play with Neil, not just piecing parts together, but like a real band. Even during Neil's long solos, like in "Cortez", the music would shift to a whole different level and we'd all go there . . . it was an idyllic time, man, Neil was just sparkling . . . I have this tape from Japan. Compared to this tape, "Zuma" sounds like a bunch of guys sleeping in big fat armchairs smoking pipes. Whenever I feel down, I listen to that tape.'

Indeed the concerts were among the most exciting Young had ever played. Looking somewhat dishevelled and playing the role of stoned buffoon to the hilt, he'd shamble on stage for an acoustic set which would take in everything from 'After The Goldrush' to 'A Man Needs A Maid' and usually end, as a sop to his fans, with 'Heart Of Gold'.

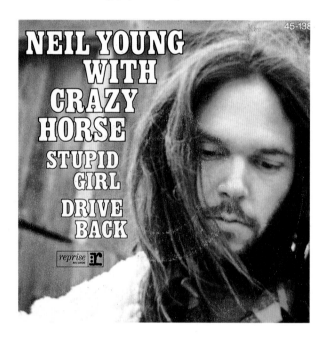

Eat a Peach

After the intermission he would return with Crazy Horse and proceed to tear the audience's heads off with a ferocious blast of electricity that would deliver the likes of 'Southern Man', 'Down By The River', 'Cinammon Girl' and 'Cortez', as well as a relentlessly driven new opus that was to become a firm favourite, 'Like A Hurricane'.

The performances effortlessly and emphatically rammed home the message that Neil Young & Crazy Horse were still one of 'the greatest bar-room bands in the world!' Sadly for Crazy Horse, their reunion with their old boss wasn't to last. Just prior to the US leg of the tour, Steve Stills persuaded Young to fly down to Miami to start work on a new project.

Neil had enjoyed an impromptu jam with Stills at UCLA's Pauley Pavilion a few months earlier. 'The spirit of the Buffalo Springfield is back!' an ecstatic Stills had hollered from the stage. It's unlikely many of the student audience were old enough to have heard or seen Buffalo Springfield, but there was an atmosphere of magic in the air. And it was perhaps predictable that Stills would be keen to recapture it by a semi-permanent reunion. The recording in Miami's Criteria Studios was successful, and Neil decided to take Stills and band out on the dates already pencilled in for Crazy Horse. The tour started in June, somewhat raggedly, but by the time it had reached Cleveland things were beginning to cook and there was most definitely a whiff of something very special in the air, particularly the moment when the ex-Springfielders wheeled into some fiery guitar work-outs.

When released with high hopes and expectations in August 1976, 'Long May You Run' was, sadly, a damp squib, subsequently meeting with poor sales and charting in the USA at a relatively paltry Number 26. Despite the apparent thrill of the pair working closely together again, and despite Neil having contributed the lion's share of the songs (including three aired on the European jaunt earlier in the year: 'Let It Shine', 'Midnight On The Bay' and 'Ocean Girl'), the results came over as lightweight when compared to the emotional highs of 'Zuma'. Only the likable title cut, a paean to Neil's old hearse Mort, and 'Fontainebleau' a vicious putdown of a Miami hotel where affluent ageing Americans go to die, cut the mustard. 'Black Coral' excepted, the Stills tunes were equally listless.

Yet, ironically, these sessions could have turned into yet another CSN&Y reunion album. Crosby and Nash, hard at work on their own magnum opus, 'Whistling Down The Wire', were interrupted by an enthused Young who suggested that the Miami recordings were going well but lacked a certain *je ne sais quoi*.

Exposure to a tape was enough to convince the duo to wing their way south to Florida and start to wrap their trademark harmonies around Stephen and Neil's lead vocals. As Graham Nash recalled on first hearing the tape and songs like 'Human Highway' and 'Black Coral': 'It sounded great, but then Neil said "Isn't there something missing?" And Crosby goes "Yeah,

Opposite: 'Stupid Girl' backed with 'Drive Back", a single from 'Zuma' which, like all of Young's post-'Harvest' 45s, failed to dent the American Top 40

Above: Neil Young's latterday status with the Nineties 'grunge' generation is not just related to his music, but to the generally unkempt look he cultivated through the Seventies and on

us," meaning me and David. We added harmonies to their existing tracks and recorded some new songs . . .'

Recording continued swiftly and successfully. One of the new songs up for consideration by the ensemble was Nash and Crosby's 'Taken At All', the lyrics to which Nash suggests were 'written about the new group situation in 1976: can this road be taken at all?' There was idle talk of turning the imminent live dates into a full-blown CSN&Y tour. Deadlines for their own album cut short further collaboration with Graham and David, and in their absence, transferring their vocals to the

safety of the master tape, Neil decided to remove them from the finished record.

Unsurprisingly Crosby and Nash were incensed by such a Machiavellian move, the ex-Hollie complaining to a Crawdaddy writer: 'Fuck 'em! They're not in it for the right reasons. They're in it for the bucks . . . the reason they wiped our voices had nothing to do with music. It had to do with whether they could have an album in time to support their tour.'

Despite the music improving night by night, by the time the tour buses rolled into Atlanta, a key member of the gang was

missing. Neil had decided, not for the first time, to cut loose, cryptically telegramming Stills with a wire that read: 'Dear Stephen, funny how things that start spontaneously end that way. Eat a peach. Neil.'

Last Waltz

Boredom? A reported throat ailment? To Neil it probably didn't matter a jot that he'd left his buddy in the lurch. As he testily asserted to *Melody Maker* years later, he's always seen himself as a law unto himself: 'I don't give a damn. Never have. Never will... no-one tells me what to do.' In retrospect, the incident appeared as yet another example of his maverick personality – when Young's had enough of something, he's not likely to stick around! Undeterred Stills shored up the remains of his band – percussionist Joe Lala, drummer Joe Vitale, bassist George Perry, keyboard player Jerry Aiello – with old Manassas member, Chris Hillman and on loan from the Eric Clapton Band, lead guitarist George Terry.

The true story behind the split, from Neil's perspective at least, was only revealed when Scott Young wrote his book. 'I was having a pretty good time,' he told his father, 'but the reviews were playing us off against each other. Stephen was reading the reviews, I was trying not to read the reviews. But even the headlines were . . . well, like "Young's hot, Stills not".

Left: Neil on stage with the 'new' Crazy Horse, featuring rhythm guitarist Frank 'Poncho' Sampedro (centre)

Above: Another 'Zuma' single. Note the B-side!

Then Stephen started thinking that other people on the tour were against him, trying to make him look bad . . . ' The bad feeling and altercations that followed were not between Stills and himself, he stressed, but ultimately had a similar effect.

Elliot Roberts conducted a damage limitation exercise, promising refunds to ticket holders or first refusal to disgruntled promoters. Neil, meanwhile, headed back to the open arms of Crazy Horse for some Californian dates and to prepare a new album tentatively called 'Chrome Dreams'. He also managed to put in an appearance at the Band's farewell concert in San Francisco at the Winterland on Thanksgiving Day, joining a veritable who's who of rock superstars: Bob Dylan, Van Morrison, Dr John, Joni Mitchell, Clapton and the Band themselves.

Martin Scorsese's subsequent celluloid rockumentary, *The Last Waltz*, captures Young playing with the Band on 'Helpless', and there is a sequence, by turns both alarming and amusing given Neil's rather puritanical public attitude to drugs, that saw the Loner gratefully accepting stimulants en route for the stage and then proceeding to play, a beatific grin across his face! In retrospect it wasn't something he was proud of, as he told *Melody Maker*:

'I was fried for *The Last Waltz*. I was on my way out, falling onstage and someone said, "Here, have some of this." I'd been up for two days, so I had some. And I was gone, you know? I'm not proud of it. I don't think people should see that and think, "Wow, that's cool." When they were editing the film, they asked me if I wanted that removed. And Robbie Robertson said, "The way you are is kinda like what the whole movie's about – if you keep on doin' this, you're just gonna die, so we're going to stop doing it" . . . I don't do it any more. I'm one of the lucky ones who was able to do that and able to stop.'

1976 was also scheduled to herald the release of 'Decade', a long-awaited triple retrospective set which Neil saw as 'a chance to use some unreleased material . . . a greatest hits album that's more like an album.' Yet on the very eve of its release, with 300,000 copies already prepared for shipment within the week, Young suddenly decided to delay its appearance and release a brand new record. It's a measure of the power Young now commanded as an artist that Warner Bros President Mo Ostin, on listening to the new material, bowed to his wishes. He'd come a long way since the first album remix problem!

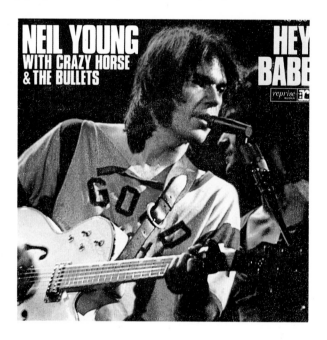

This new album, christened 'American Stars'n'Bars' ('because one side is about American folk heroes and the other is about getting loose in bars') was considerably different to the one Young had originally planned to release. The 'draft' version had contained such songs as 'Captain Kennedy' (to appear later on 'Hawks And Doves'), 'Pocohontas', 'Powderfinger' and 'Sedan Delivery' (which would appear on 'Rust Never Sleeps').

The two last-named songs had been offered to Lynyrd Skynyrd for their 'Street Survivors' set, but never used, and thereby hangs a tale.

Skynyrd had written their anthemic 'Sweet Home Alabama' as a riposte to Young's 'Southern Man', but a sense of mutual respect had since grown up between Neil and the southerners. Sadly Neil never got to meet their lead singer Ronnie Van Zant,

one of three band members killed that October in a plane crash – and, sadly, Van Zant never realised his ambition to record a solo version of 'Powderfinger'.

Getting Loaded

Young spent the first months of 1977 remoulding 'Stars'n'Bars' which, when it emerged in May, boasted a different selection of tunes, much more oriented towards a celebration of the hedonistic lifestyle than a tribute to all-American heroes he'd originally planned. Dean Stockwell's sleeve artwork has all the clues, especially the back cover with its honky-tonk woman, empty bottle of liquor and Young's wasted expression. Getting loaded was the key to Neil's current direction. It was a period of enjoying life and drinking for the fun of it rather than to hide any pain – a notion reinforced by the sloppy feel to some of the tracks.

The first side is a clutch of songs fresh out of the hen house ('written fast and in the spirit of country music'), performed by Crazy Horse with the sweet steel of Ben Keith and sawing fiddle of Carole Mayedo and sweetened by the crooning of the Saddlebags (Linda Ronstadt & Nicolette Larsen). 'Old Country Waltz', 'Saddle Up The Palomino' and 'Hold Back The Tears' saw Neil at his most countrified: *Melody Maker*'s review listed his concerns as 'contradictory attitudes to women, love and its defeats and

Above: A single taken from 'American Stars And Bars' betrays that album's piecemeal nature by its very credits

Right: Getting down with Billy Talbot

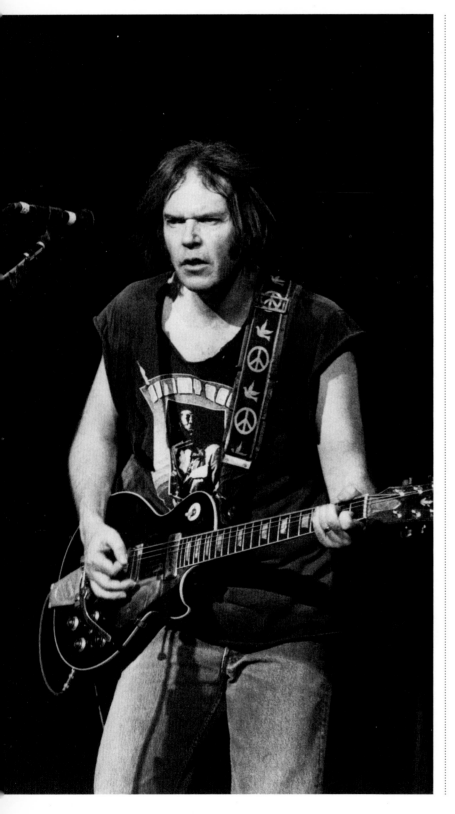

cruel disappointments . . . marked by a melancholic despair and resignation, made tolerable by the weary humour and stubborn resilience that Young invariably introduces.'

The second side was rather less straightforward, consisting of a mish-mash of older tracks ranging from the fragile 'Star Of Bethlehem', a ballad from the lost 'Homegrown' sessions of November 1974 where Young duetted with Emmylou Harris, to a couple of more toothsome workouts with Crazy Horse. Most notable of these was the already legendary 'Like A Hurricane', an ode to a bar in Redwood City, California, which made it on to vinyl at last. Subsequently regarded as one of the highlights of Neil's long career, this version never quite reaches the epic grandeur of 'Cortez The Killer' to which it has often been favourably compared.

This may be on account of the trite lyrics ('I am just a dreamer and you are just a dream') or perhaps because his guitar solo fails to break free of Sampedro's smothering mellotron (cuttingly dismissed as being reminiscent of King Crimson by a vicious Nick Kent in *NME*). 'Homegrown', wherein Neil extols the virtues of DIY among dope smokers, closes proceedings on something of a throwaway not but catching Crazy Horse all revved up, their electric guitars crackling and spitting in vintage fashion.

The Ducks

On that evidence, it's a shame that another Crazy Horse cut wasn't included here to replace the excruciatingly long and maudlin 'Will To Love'. This drove Nick Kent, in the same *NME* review, to bitch: '(it) may well be the worst song Young's ever written . . . a horribly trite acoustic minor-chord affair that America wouldn't even dare to put on one of their albums!'

Left: Neil with his familiar peace-sign-and-doves guitar strap

Opposite: The Japanese release of 'Heart Of Gold' coupled with 'Only Love Can Break Your Heart'

It was Young's quest for the pleasures in life which led him briefly into a very unusual but extremely rewarding situation, a stint as lead guitarist for a Santa Cruz-based outfit, the Ducks. For the first time in ten years, Young was in a set-up where the spotlight was not focused on him alone and, with the pressures off, he rose regally to the occasion. The Ducks' line-up initially consisted of Eddie Harris on guitar, drummer John Craviotta (also known as Johnny C, an ex-sideman of Ry Cooder), singer-guitar player Jeff Blackburn and bass-man Bob Mosley, both of whom Neil had known from his Springfield days.

Mosley had been in the original line-up of San Francisco's wild and notorious acid-rockers, Moby Grape, while Blackburn had cut some impressive sides for Verve as one part of the folk-rock duo Blackburn & Snow (with Sherri Snow, who later resurfaced in Dan Hicks and His Hot Licks). The pair had been playing around the coastal resort in various com-

binations for several years, including a later line-up of the Grape with Craviotta.

When Harris quit, Young – who happened to be visiting Blackburn – was offered the now-vacant job and joined the Ducks, who were being managed by another Young alumnus: Jim Mazzeo had provided the artwork for the 'Zuma' sleeve and received a namecheck on the 'Stars'n'Bars' album. According to *BAM* magazine, the Ducks had taken their name from an incident in local folklore in which a surfer by the name of Pussinger, out driving around the Twin Lakes area, had flattened eight ducks and sent local wildfowlers into uproar over the senseless killings.

Pussinger was given eight days in jail – one day for each of the ducks he had killed – after which he gave up surfing and headed for the comparative safety of Happy Camp up in the Sierras. Meanwhile, Santa Cruz was left with the 'Pussinger Curse', which could only be lifted by the Ducks playing in as many bars as possible and getting their audiences to furiously quack along on duck calls!

Young rented a beach house for rehearsals and the combo were soon a hot act around local clubs such as the Catalyst, the Crossroads and the Backroom. Neil was particularly happy with the laid-back situation, observing: 'This band isn't just me and some other guys who back me up. I just play my part. It kind of reminds me of when I was in the Buffalo Springfield. It feels good to be a part of this group, like being in a band for the first time!'

Indeed, their eclectic repertoire would feature a stirring 'Mr Soul' in among Chuck Berry numbers, a hot cover of 'Gone Dead Train' and songs from the pens of Mosley and Blackburn, including Mosley's hard rock masterpiece 'Gypsy Wedding' (the opening salvo on Moby Grape's '20 Granite Creek' album from 1971) and the soulful 'Said It Ain't No Secret'. These contrasted beautifully with some of Blackburn's more lyrical country-tinged efforts like 'Two Riders', 'Sky Blue' and the showstopping 'Silver Wings'.

Into this heady brew Young added his five cents' worth – raw versions of 'Long May You Run' and 'Are You Ready For The Country' and some new material like 'Comes A Time', 'Cryin' Eyes' and the set closer 'Windward Passage' that has never appeared on record. A stunning instrumental worthy of early

NEIL YOUNG as he appears in "THE LAST WALTZ".

JONI MITCHELL as she appears in "THE LAST WALTZ".

Above: Winnipeg's most famous musical exports, Neil Young and Joni Mitchell, featured on promotional material for the movie 'The Last Waltz'

Quicksilver Messenger Service, it took the twin-guitar work-outs of Crazy Horse a step further and in its simplicity even owed a debt to one of Young's all-time heroes, British Shadows guitarist Hank B. Marvin!

End of the Fairytale

For the summer months, Joe Public could pay a coupla bucks and see Young burning up the frets of his black Gibson Les Paul emblazoned with the legend, Santa Cruz, in an intimate club atmosphere. Unfortunately once the word got out, the curiosity-seekers, journalists and even record company personnel started to show up and the thrill was gone. Neil left town after his house was burgled; the Ducks continued with an open invitation for him to rejoin whenever he felt like it – a second ex-Grape renegade, Jerry Miller, being one of several subsequent replacements.

Talking about his involvement with Young 18 months later, Jeff Blackburn was suitably philosophical: 'It's almost hard to comprehend it ever happened. We all knew that Neil had his commitments and everything . . . I guess we were all in the fairytale and unable to see out of it.'

Frustratingly, nothing has ever surfaced on record to document this short but fruitful period of Young's career. However in December 1977, *Melody Maker* tantalised Neil's fans with a snippet that a double album recorded on Neil's remote 16-track unit was imminent which 'includes new and old material by Young in addition to contributions from the band's two other songwriters . . .'

Such a work would have been a veritable eye-opener, Young's voice meshing with the tonsils of Blackburn and Mosley to create powerful harmonies, while his sparkling lead guitar lines added that extra touch of magic to his compadres'

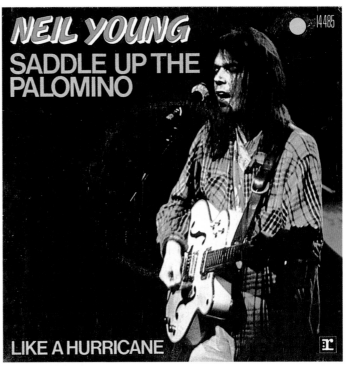

own songs. Bob Mosley, meanwhile, would later be considered for the bassist's position in the 'Trans' band which went in the end to Bruce Palmer.

Following a spontaneous appearance with Crosby and Nash at the Civic Auditorium, where he was allowed to perform three of his own songs – 'New Mama', 'Only Love Can Break Your Heart' and, surprisingly, 'Sugar Mountain', a tune not normally associated with CSN&Y – Young quit the Santa Cruz scene altogether, and with his son Zeke in tow, drove his tour bus south.

He ended up in Nashville where he decided to record his next album. Using a core of C&W session men, unaccustomed to playing rock, he called upon Nicolette Larsen once more for harmony vocals and recruited six additional acoustic guitarists. Christening this aggregation the Gone With The Wind Orchestra, Young rehearsed them in a Nashville storefront

and, to celebrate his 32nd birthday, flew the lot down to Florida for an outdoor benefit in aid of children's hospitals in the Miami Beach area. It was to be their only public appearance, the concert – attended by 125,000 people – climaxing with 'Sweet Home Alabama' which he dedicated to 'a couple of friends in the sky'.

Due to pressing problems, the fruits of this collaboration took a whole year to surface as 'Comes A Time'. When it did, it was immediately applauded by many for its warm atmosphere and for an accessibility not demonstrated since 'Harvest'. The presence of JJ Cale, king of the sleepy laid-back guitar, gives a hint as to what was to be expected. It was for the most part an acoustic opus, *Melody Maker* declaring it: '"American Stars'n'Bars" without the electricity.' Even the two tracks with Crazy Horse saw them 'unplugged' and low-key, the one exception being an aggressive, fuzz-guitar-led blues track called 'Motorcycle Mama'.

Though the much anticipated 'Human Highway' was dusted off, it's the cover of Ian Tyson's old chestnut 'Four Strong Winds' (a nod back to his formative days in Canada?) that proved the winning cut. An elegant ballad about a collapsing relationship, it was sensibly pulled out as a single and charted at Number 61 in the US, and 57 in Great Britain. Never one to conform to his audience's expectations, Neil had gone and cut what was to all intents and purposes a folk album – and at the height of punk, too! Despite accusations of blandness, 'Comes A Time' was to be his best-selling album release since 'Harvest', reaching Number 7 in the US and 42 in the UK.

Vintage Young

The much-delayed triple album 'Decade' eventually came out in December. Despite the timing of its release ensuring it made a mighty large lump in Christmas stockings the world over, it was no record company marketing stunt but a genuine comprehensive history of Neil's artistic development. As the title suggested, it encapsulated Young's best work over the preceding ten years from Buffalo Springfield, CSN&Y and solo, along with previously unreleased material.

Nicely packaged and expertly compiled by Young, Tim Mulligan and David Briggs, it finally anthologised the popular live song 'Sugar Mountain' that had previously languished on the B-side of numerous singles. But given the amount of unissued material in Young's personal archives, 'Decade' was disappointingly low on unreleased gems.

'Down To The Wire' was an alluring tidbit to delight Buffalo Springfield fans, while Young's own version of 'Love Is A Rose' (better known as a track by Linda Ronstadt) was finally vinylised, with only three remaining tunes unreleased. Nevertheless these – 'Winterlong', 'Deep Forbidden Lake' (from the 'Homegrown' sessions) and 'Campaigner' – would all be described by *Melody Maker* as 'vintage Young'.

The last-named was arguably the most interesting of the three tracks. It was originally known as 'Requiem For A President', written one afternoon during the Stills-Young Band tour. Young, sitting quietly watching the TV news in his manager's hotel room, was suddenly presented on the screen with the image of a haggard, emotional Richard Nixon visiting his paralysed wife, Pat, in hospital. Young retired to the tour bus and hours later, on

Above: The standout cut from 'American Stars And Bars', 'Like A Hurricane' has inspired covers from both Roxy Music and the Mission. Pictured here is the German release

Right: The wind machine blows up a storm on stage

Overleaf: With David Crosby (insert) and his ever-faithful steed Crazy Horse

Tricky Dicky? No, Neil Young fooling around in the Seventies!

He wrote 'Campaigner' about the discredited ex-president,

admitting he'd pitied the once-vilified Nixon

stage, played the song he'd just written, which contained the memorable stanza:

> *Hospitals have made him cry*
> *But there's always a freeway in his eye*
> *Though his beach got too crowded for a stroll*
> *Roads stretch out like healthy veins*
> *And wild gift horses strain the reins*
> *Where even Richard Nixon has got soul*

The politician whose actions had once provoked Neil Young to write one of the Seventies' most potent anti-violence songs, 'Ohio', was here touching a different nerve; as the singer observed in an article in *Rolling Stone*, 'Guess I felt sorry for (Nixon) that night.'

As the festive season came around, Young's short-lived romantic liaison with singer Nicolette Larsen ended, and in the aftermath he renewed his friendship with neighbour, Pegi Morton. Courtship then began in earnest and eight months later the couple were married, honeymooning on Neil's yacht *WN Ragland*. It was a significant first step towards building a new family unit that would play a crucial role in Young's life in the years to come.

Human Highway

The scars from his ill-fated first film, *Journey Through The Past*, had obviously healed sufficiently for Young to consider embarking on a new project in the opening months of 1978. Variously described as 'documentary-style Western' and a 'comedy/fantasy/musical', it was given a working title of *Human Highway*. Dean Stockwell, the original inspiration for 'After The Goldrush', had come back into the frame to star in and direct the film, while Dennis Hopper was signed to head the cast.

In the course of their discussions, Stockwell turned Neil on to New Wave avant-gardists Devo. Instinctively the singer knew that the band would be just right for a planned nightmare sequence in the film, and quickly had them flown in from their Akron, Ohio, headquarters. They were filmed at San Francisco's prime punk nightspot, the Mabuhay Gardens, performing a new composition entitled 'Out Of The Blue'; Young had co-written the song with Ducks cohort Jeff Blackburn with the Sex Pistols in mind.

While his contemporaries had chosen to ignore or deride the new music sweeping through the business, Young, always the maverick that he was, characteristically welcomed the winds of change being stirred up by punk rock. Having already picked up on its first rumblings in London back in the spring of 1976, he saw that even if much of it was merely a case of the emperor's new clothes, punk was determined to blow away the

climate of stagnation and challenge rock'n'roll's complacency. And he saw the new bands very much as kindred spirits.

During a private show at the Mabuhay Gardens, Devo executed the planned piece and introduced Young onstage as 'Granpa Granola'; they also threw in a hideous parody of 'After The Goldrush', seemingly very much to Neil's perverse taste. A take of 'Out Of The Blue' was also done in a local studio, during which members of Devo chanted a bizarre phrase, 'rust never sleeps', that struck a chord in the guitarist's imagination. Mark Mothersbaugh, Devo's leader, had a background in advertising and had thought up the expression as part of a campaign to sell Rustoleum, a rust remover. Devo felt it fitted

Frank Sampedro (left) proved an admirable on-stage foil for Young, although he could never fully replace the sadly departed Danny Whitten as the motivating force of Crazy Horse

the mood of the song, while Young felt it was the perfect metaphor for his career and his constant battle to keep his muse alive.

Further footage was shot in late May when Young booked into the Bottom Line club in New York to perform eight solo concerts, during which he experimented with a concealed wireless microphone that allowed him to roam around in the club wherever he chose. Now retitled 'My My Hey Hey (Out Of

Above: Long-time bass guitarist with Crazy Horse Billy Talbot duets with Neil

Right: Stephen Stills, with David Crosby in the background, reunites once again with on-and-off partner of twenty years standing Neil Young

Opposite: A surrealist-looking scene from *Rust Never Sleeps*, a much-maligned and misunderstood movie which co-starred the eccentric Akron new wave band Devo and the eerily-hooded Road-eyes seen here

The Blue)', the new song was an integral part of a set of songs largely unfamiliar to his followers. (Some were to appear on the delayed 'Comes A Time'; others, like 'Shots', would have to wait until 1981's 'Re.Ac.Tor'.)

Inspired by punk's young pretenders, Young suddenly dropped his film plans in the summer to return to the road with Crazy Horse and indulge in some raunchy rabble-rousing rock'n'roll. This was good news to messrs Talbot, Molina and Sampedro, who had been treading water on their projected fourth solo effort, begun back in 1975 at Zuma Beach. This record was finally completed in August, the trio augmented by

ex-Rocket Bobby Notkoff on violin, Rockets producer Barry Goldberg on piano, Greg Leroy on guitar and Mike Curtis on synth. Released that November on RCA, 'Crazy Moon' proved their most realised work to date, smoking with good time rock'n'raunch.

With Sampedro revelling in his Little Richard and Chuck Berry roots, they kicked up a storm on numbers like 'She's Hot' and 'Thunder And Lightning'. The band were joined by their boss for half the cuts and his stinging leads imbued songs like 'Downhill' with a 'Zuma'-esque magic, his presence prompting Sampedro to reminisce: 'I was real timid of Neil

during the "Zuma" sessions, but when we got to (Young's) ranch and started working on some of our songs, I found myself leading Neil!'

The six weeks of US shows culminated in a series of sell-out nights at Madison Square Gardens, New York City. Known as the 'Rust Never Sleeps' tour, it was intended to shoot dates for a less ambitious film of the same name, scripted and directed by film-makers LA Johnson and Jeanne Field. The concerts used elaborate backdrops and props – gigantic packing cases, amplifiers, microphones and even an outsize Marine Band harmonica. These were all constructed right in front of the

audience's noses by the road crew, now dubbed Road-eyes and dressed in cowls lit by burning red eyes that recalled the Jawas from *Star Wars*, one of Neil's favourite films.

As the stage was readied, the assembled fans were serenaded by a tape of Hendrix's 'Star-spangled Banner' and the Beatles' 'A Day In The Life'. More tellingly, Young chose to intersperse these with stage announcements from the *Woodstock* soundtrack – taken out of context, they sounded almost laughable. Another indication that Young wanted to distance himself from the peace'n'love Sixties associations that were still very much a part of the CS&N image? A message to the New Wavers that he wasn't burnt out yet but still a creative force to be reckoned with?

The singer once again upset the expectant fans, there to hear the syrupy ballads from the just-released 'Comes A Time', by playing a show that ended with an extended, Crazy Horse-backed set that was an ear-melting heavy metal *pièce de résistance*. Bouncing around the stage and tearing it up like a deranged pinhead was yet another slap in the face of fans who still regarded their hero as the romantic singer-songwriter figure of the early Seventies, the once self-styled 'Loner'. These shows were proving that Young took neither the image of himself nor the machinations of the music biz too seriously.

If 1978 saw Young rising to new artistic heights and happily married, it ended in a double tragedy. His house on Zuma Beach was destroyed on 23 October, caught up in the forest fires that ravaged the Southern Californian coastline. And then in November, his second son, Ben, was born and subsequently diagnosed as suffering from cerebral palsy. It was an incredible, heartbreaking coincidence – Neil's first son, Zeke, born to him and Carrie Snodgress, also suffered from a milder form of the disease. Specialists at the Stanford Hospital in Palo Alto diagnosed Ben as a spastic, quadriplegic and non-oral child. Young immediately had himself checked over, but the medics assured him that the condition was non-hereditary, the odds against its afflicting both children massive.

Rust Never Sleeps

While the Youngs tried to come to terms with this crushing bolt from the blue, *Rust Never Sleeps*, the film, premiered in LA on 11 July 1979 (credited to director Bernard Shakey, Young's alter ego), simultaneous with the worldwide release of the first of two projected albums chronicling this era. *Rust* the movie had been pared down to nothing more than concert footage that was shot on the night of 22 October 1978 at San Francisco's Cow Palace and contained no revealing backstage interviews with Young, concentrating solely on what was going down out front.

'Rust Never Sleeps', the album (US 8/UK 13), consisted of an acoustic side (with the ubiquitous Nicolette Larsen on vocals, Joe Osborne on bass guitar and drummer Karl Himmel) and an electric side (on which he was backed by Crazy Horse), the record opening and closing with variations on the 'My My Hey Hey' song, which ruminated on the fleeting nature of rock'n'roll stardom. In between were sandwiched a strong collection of tunes.

Among the exceptional cuts on the acoustic side were 'Pocohontas', inspired by the sight of Sasheen Whitefeather collecting Marlon Brando's Oscar for his role in *The Godfather*, that saw Young returning again to the theme of the destruction of the indigenous people of North America (first explored on 'Broken Arrow') and the impressive 'Thrasher', which many have seen as a veiled commentary on his relationship with Crosby, Stills and Nash.

The real meat of 'Rust' was in the four scorching electric numbers that boil up Side 2. 'Powderfinger', a Western tale of a teenage boy's simultaneous coming of age and his come-uppance at the hands of river pirates, was narrated over the familiar chug of Crazy Horse's engine room, a thick mist of guitars intermittently punctuated by Young's belligerent lead lines. 'Sedan Delivery' and 'Welfare Mothers' whirled the listener into a maelstrom of heavy metal over which mocked

Crosby Stills Nash and Young could always fill stadia purely by turning up, a concept one suspects was anathema to Young's creative urge. Here they play such a venue in 1978

Young's wilfully surreal lyrics. A second blast of the album's theme song followed, this time entitled 'Hey Hey My My (Into The Black)', Molina's whiplash percussion assailing the ears as the song pitched into heavy industrial noise a million miles removed from the mellowness of 'Comes A Time'. The guitar solos were of speaker-blowing intensity as the song built up to a hysterical climax, Young's scream 'Is this the story of Johnny Rotten ?' answered by Crazy Horse's bellowing chorus of 'Rotten Johnny, Rotten Johnny'.

If the album generally met with a critical thumbs-up, then its impact was lessened by the arrival, four months later, of 'Live Rust'. The general consensus was that this double album (US 15/UK 55) – the soundtrack to the film – had nothing new to say, especially in the light of the superb 'Decade' set. And, worse, it was a blatant exercise in exploiting his fans, Melody Maker accusing it of being 'merely an expensive way of marking time'. With no new material and a less-than-vital opening side of familiar old acoustic songs, 'Live Rust' was further damned by an idiotic reggae version of 'Cortez The Killer' with Young singing the final verse in a cod imitation of a West Indian accent. It was left to 'Cinnamon Girl' and 'Like A Hurricane' to inject some idea of the live excitement.

The critical backlash that met 'Live Rust' closed what, for Young, had been a decade of great artistic achievement – he was one of precious few stars (like Dylan and Van Morrison) who had survived the volatile Seventies with his integrity intact. He could at least take comfort in Village Voice nominating him as 'Artist of the Decade'. More intriguingly, as Young had intimated to Rolling Stone writer Cameron Crowe, he was already preparing himself for the next decade:

'The Eighties are here. I've got to just tear down whatever has happened to me and build something new. You can only have it for so long before you don't have it any more. You become an old timer . . . which I could be . . . I don't know.' So reinventing himself became the name of Neil's game in the 1980s.

Time Fades Away (1973)

Young's first live album – a document of the gruelling US tour that covered sixty-five cities in early 1973, and which was beset by personnel and musical problems – and the first in a succession that would see the singer trying to come to terms with the massive success of his 'Heart of Gold' hit. There was no disputing the calibre of his back-up band, the Stray Gators – Tim Drummond, Johnny Barbata, Ben Keith and Jack Nitzsche – but the LP drips with the overwhelming frustration Young was then enduring, playing large, 20,000-seater venues, and his inability to draw out of the Gators the precise sound he had in his head. Not even the harmony vocals of Crosby and Nash could sweeten the pill.

The hooks and laid-back groove that made his previous work, 'Harvest' so accessible had been replaced by a fierce urgency, but despite its flaws 'Time' contained several important additions to the Young canon such as 'The Bridge' and the strikingly autobiographical 'Don't Be Denied'.

Track listing:

Time Fades Away • Journey Thru The Past • Yonder Stands The Sinner • LA • Love In Mind • Don't Be Denied • The Bridge • Last Dance

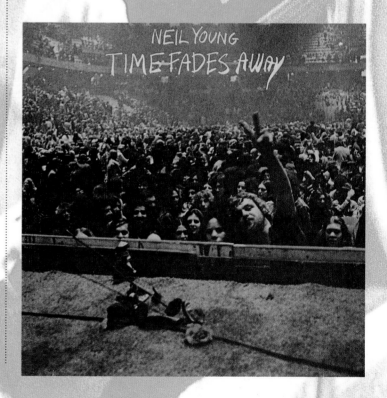

On The Beach (1974)

Released in preference to 'Tonight's The Night' and therefore chronologically out of sequence, 'Beach' caught Young in a sombre, depressed state of mind. On one level it reflected the singer's growing disillusionment with his own position and superstardom and his increasing disenchantment with the lifestyles of the pampered media stars who inhabited his world, no better embodied than on 'Revolution Blues' on which he tried to exorcise these demons by assuming the guise of murderer Charles Manson.

On another, it sees Young finally realising that the naive but optimistic hopes and dreams of the Sixties were sadly crumbling all around. The long final track, 'Ambulance Blues', echoed the despair of Bob Dylan's 'Desolation Row', but was more direct with Young staring into the void, concluding that life adds up to a big fat zero in the line 'You're all just pissin' in the wind'.

Track listing:

Walk On • See The Sky About To Rain • Revolution Blues • For The Turnstiles • Vampire Blues • On The Beach • Motion Pictures • Ambulance Blues

So Far
(with Crosby, Stills & Nash) (1974)

Not unlike the double eponymously titled Buffalo Springfield retrospective that was released in 1973 to capitalise on Neil Young's burgeoning solo success, 'So Far' was little more than an opportunistic attempt by the record company to cash in on the (albeit temporary) reformation of the supergroup. Crosby, Stills, Nash and Young were originally planning to release an album of new material, the working title of which was 'Human Highway', before personal friction during the recording sessions consigned the whole project to the studio waste bin.

The collection is notable only in that it anthologised both sides of 1970's single, 'Ohio' and featured specially commissioned artwork by long time Neil Young friend and admirer, fellow Canadian Joni Mitchell.

Track listing:

Deja Vu • Helplessly Hoping • Wooden Ships • Teach Your Children • Ohio • Find The Cost Of Freedom • Woodstock • Our House • Helpless • Guenevere • Judy Blue Eyes

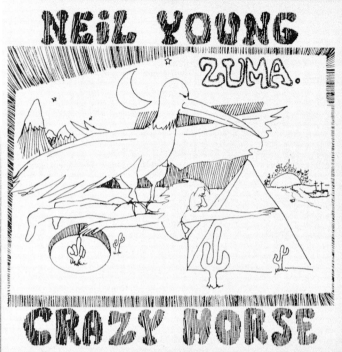

Tonight's The Night (1975)

Recorded in 1973 in the emotional fall-out surrounding the drug-related deaths of two of his closest friends, Danny Whitten and Bruce Berry, 'Tonight' emerged two years later as one of rock music's most unremittingly grim oeuvres, made tolerable only by the 'blood'n'guts' passion with which Young and company (an expanded Crazy Horse including Nils Lofgren) set about recording it. Although apparently softened by the later addition of two new songs, 'Lookout Joe' and 'New Mama', this album remained totally uncompromising, the sessions for it taking the musicians right to the edge as they sought the right level of energy and intensity of feeling to do justice to the muse created by their departed friends.

Young would later describe it as 'a wake' and there's a real sense of the album acting as a means of purging the sense of guilt and failed responsibility which he obviously felt over their deaths.

Track listing:

Tonight's The Night • Speakin' Out • World On A String • Borrowed Tune • Come On Baby • Let's Go Down-Town • Mellow My Mind • Roll Another Number (For The Road) • Albuquerque • New Mama • Look Out, Joe • Tired Eyes • Tonight's The Night (Part 2)

Zuma (1975)

Celebrating his reunion with a revamped Crazy Horse, Frank Sampedro replacing the departed Danny Whitten, 'Zuma' was both a nod back to his well-received second and third albums and anticipated the tougher stance of late-Seventies work like 'Rust Never Sleeps'. Upbeat, commercial tunes such as 'Don't Cry No Tears' and 'Lookin' For A Love' (released as a single) came as a relief to fans upset by the difficult trio of LPs that preceded it. 'Stupid Girl' and 'Danger Bird' were hard rockers whose scorching guitar sound would elicit praise from ex-Velvet Underground singer Lou Reed.

The undoubted highlight was the extended 'Cortez The Killer', the first in a number of songs that would show Young's fascination with the ancient Aztec/Inca civilisations and one boasting stunning lead guitar work seldom heard since 'Everybody Knows This Is Nowhere'. The album closed with the acoustic 'Through My Sails', a CSN&Y cut from the aborted 1973 Maui rehearsals.

Track listing:

Don't Cry No Tears • Danger Bird • Pardon My Heart • Lookin' For A Love • Barstool Blues • Stupid Girl • Drive Back • Cortez The Killer • Through My Sails

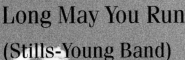

Long May You Run

(Stills-Young Band) (1976)

Almost a full-blown Crosby, Stills, Nash and Young reunion until the deadlines for their own album forced Crosby and Nash to abandon the recordings, and Young wiped out their backing vocals, 'Long May You Run' came as something of a disappointment – especially to those who had taken to heart Stills' comment, 'The spirit of the Buffalo Springfield is back' when he and Young had jammed live in LA and first floated the idea of collaboration.

Of the five Young originals, only the title track, a tune that was inspired by Mort his old hearse, and 'Fontainebleau' (a curiously vitriolic attack on a Miami hotel and its occupants), bore serious repeated listening. Stephen Stills' contributions fared no better: somehow, the on-stage fire that had been rekindled just didn't materialise down at Miami's Criteria Studios.

Track listing:

Long May You Run • Make Love To You • Midnight On The Bay • Black Coral • Ocean Girl • Let It Shine • 12/8 Blues • Fontainebleau • Guardian Angel

American Stars and Bars (1977)

This much tinkered-with recording project started life as the aborted 'Chrome Dreams' and then changed direction, the idea being to feature on the one side a celebration of various American folk heroes, and on the other – in a somewhat bizarre pairing – a celebration of US bar culture. When it finally surfaced, 'Stars'n'Bars' was a mixture of very new and older material, but in the main a hymn to the pleasures of getting 'blitzed'.

Side 1 boasts five country numbers backed up by Crazy Horse, fiddler Carole Mayedo and the Saddlebags, Nicolette Larsen and Linda Ronstadt, on harmony vocals; the result was certainly fun if not particularly vital.

The second side contained the older tracks and for the most part continued the drinking theme, climaxing magnificently with the much anticipated 'Like A Hurricane', that has been a major highlight of live appearances by Neil Young before and since.

Track listing:

Old Country Waltz • Saddle Up The Palomino • Hey Babe • Hold Back The Tears • Bite The Bullet • Star Of Bethlehem • Will To Live • Like A Hurricane • Homegrown

Decade (1977)

A yardstick by which all other greatest hits compilations should be measured, 'Decade' was a three-disc set put together by the maestro himself that covered most of his musical activities from Buffalo Springfield onward, the first side pulling together Young's major contributions to that band plus the bonus of an unreleased track. The solo years were well represented – classic material with backing by Crazy Horse, the title track from the Stills-Young Band fiasco and a further five unreleased tracks, most notable being 'Campaigner', an ode to Richard Nixon, the US president who had inspired 'Ohio'.

Track listing:

Down To The Wire • Burned • Mr Soul • Broken Arrow • Expecting To Fly • Sugar Mountain • I Am A Child • The Loner • The Old Laughing Lady • Cinnamon Girl • Down By The River • Cowgirl In The Sand • I Believe In You • After The Goldrush • Southern Man • Helpless • Ohio • Soldier • Old Man • Man Needs A Maid • Heart Of Gold • Star Of Bethlehem • The Needle And The Damage Done • Tonight's The Night (Part 1) • Turnstiles • Winterlong • Deep Forbidden Lake • Like A Hurricane • Love Is A Rose • Cortez The Killer • Campaigner • Long May You Run • Harvest

Comes A Time (1978)

Manufacturing problems delayed the release of this mellow set recorded in autumn 1977 in Nashville with the Gone With The Wind Orchestra, and fans subsequently found it hard to equate the soon-to-arrive 'Rust Never Sleeps' incarnation of their hero with the melodic music here. It became Young's best-selling album since 'Harvest', and both works wallow in a similarly relaxed atmosphere – the presence of guitarist JJ Cale, celebrated for his laid-back approach, contributed to this mood. Young was again joined by Nicolette Larsen, whose silky harmony vocals add much warmth to songs like the title cut, 'Human Highway' and 'Goin' Back'.

The overall rosy glow is further enhanced by the string and acoustic guitar textures, especially on the old folk chestnut, Ian Tyson's 'Four Strong Winds', that became the album's single. Only 'Motorcycle Mama', a long fuzz-guitar dominated blues, disrupts the sunny feel.

Track listing:

Goin' Back • Comes A Time • Look Out For My Love • Peace Of Mind • Lotta Love • Human Highway • Already One • Field Of Opportunity • Motor Cycle Mama • Four Strong Winds

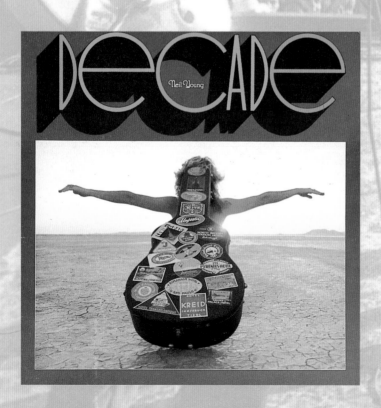

Rust Never Sleeps   (1979)

'Rust', Young's final studio album of the Seventies, saw him drawing inspiration from the punk revolution yapping at the heels of rock's pantheon – and in doing so found him attempting to avoid the creative stagnation that many of his contemporaries from the Sixties were suffering. The title came from a phrase once used in an advertising campaign by his friends and collaborators, Devo, and Young seized upon it as the perfect metaphor for his continuing struggle to keep his music fresh and alive. Side 1 of 'Rust' was a collection of neo-acoustic songs including 'My My Hey Hey (Out Of The Blue)' which ruminated on the transience of rock stardom. But it was the electric maelstrom of the flipside which really represented the album's true heart. Accompanied by the ever-faithful Crazy Horse, Young blasted his way through four storming numbers that left followers of great rock'n'roll in no doubt that he was still a force to be reckoned with.

Track listing:

My My Hey Hey (Out Of The Blue) • Thrasher • Ride My Llama • Pocohontas • Sail Away • Powder Finger • Welfare Mothers • Sedan Delivery • Hey Hey My My (Into The Black)

Live Rust

(Neil Young & Crazy Horse)   (1979)

This double live album, soundtrack to the *Rust Never Sleeps* movie, was less than enthusiastically received. With the release of the film on video, it became easier to appreciate, for without the aid of the visuals 'Live Rust' is little more than a memento of Young and Crazy Horse's autumn 1978 tour, recorded at San Francisco's Cow Palace on 22 October. It offers no new songs, with one acoustic and three electric sides of familiar material that reach some notable lows – the 'reggae' version of 'Cortez The Killer' a case in point.

More disappointingly it closed on a negative note a decade that had seen Young reach a position of artistic excellence shared only by his mentor, Bob Dylan.

Track listing:

Sugar Mountain • I Am A Child • Comes A Time • After The Goldrush • My My Hey Hey (Out Of The Blue) • When You Dance I Can Really Love You • The Loner • The Needle And The Damage Done • Lotta Love • Sedan Delivery • Powder Finger • Cortez The Killer • Cinnamon Girl • Like A Hurricane • Hey Hey My My (Into The Black) • Tonight's The Night

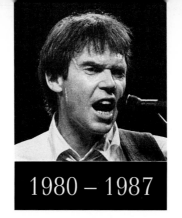

1980 – 1987

A Period of Transition

To his ever-growing legion of fans, Neil Young must have looked like one of rock's invincible warriors as the turbulent Eighties began, exuding a confidence that bordered on the arrogant. Take, for example, his dismissive response when asked whether he would submit to yet another reunion with CS&N. 'Who cares?' Young quipped. 'It's better for them to remember it the way it was. That's why Muhammad Ali isn't fighting anymore.'

Yet unbeknown to all but his intimate circle of family and friends, Neil was far from preoccupied with matters musical. The first two years of the new decade were to be taken up with the care of young son, Ben. Neil and wife Pegi approached the Institute for Achievement of Human Potential in Philadelphia, a body which assisted parents of handicapped children to give them a chance in life they might not otherwise have.

While waiting to find out if their application to join the Institute's program was to be accepted, tragedy struck the couple yet again when Pegi was diagnosed as suffering a very serious neurological condition and given only a 50/50 chance of recovery. Fortunately her subsequent operation was a com-

plete success and she was soon recuperating aboard their yacht WN Ragland, the Young family spending the summer sailing around the southern Pacific. But the whole episode must have made him question once again life's cruel capriciousness and why he, in particular, had been singled out by another extreme quirk of fate.

Despite his time-consuming family commitments, Neil found time to continue work on his *Human Highway* film. At around the same time, producer David Briggs (responsible for putting together the soundtrack) asked him to contribute to another movie – *Where The Buffalo Roam*, based on the life of writer Hunter S. Thompson. He duly obliged with not one but seven gonzoid, mainly instrumental variations of 'Home On The Range', complete with screaming guitar lines the maverick Thompson must totally have approved of! The Youngs were subsequently accepted by the Institute, but their commitment to it was to be all-consuming: they had to give themselves over to it 12 hours a day, seven days a week.

A 'Trans'-era Young uses his vocoder to blast out unearthly vocal effects in a period that alienated many and saw him roundly booed by unhappy German fans

The early '80s were a time of all-consuming family commitments for Young as he and his wife worked with their son Ben – music became a rare but much-needed relief

The airy 'Hawks & Doves' contained songs such as 'Coastline' and 'Stayin' Power' which reflected the new-found dedication of his domestic lifestyle

'It was an almost Nazi kind of programme,' Young would later comment. 'They had us doing these things that didn't help our child, but they had us convinced that if we didn't do the programme, we were not doing the right thing for the kid. And it kept us busy all the working hours of the day, seven days a week, until the kid was better. We had no time to ourselves. Can you imagine what that's like? We couldn't leave the house. We had to be there doing this programme, and it was an excruciatingly difficult thing for the kid to go through because he was crying almost all day, it was so hard. We did it a couple of years before we just couldn't do it anymore.'

Ben began his progress on the Institute's programme in October, almost concurrently with the release of his dad's new

album, 'Hawks & Doves', most of which had been recorded in Hollywood during the preceding months. It had a country, airy feel to it, a stark contrast to the 'all-guns-blazing' Crazy Horse outings of 1979; in the light of this, it was dismissed by some on account of its lightweight musical accompaniment.

Shadow, Rider and Birds

The ubiquitous Ben Keith was back on steel guitar, Tim Drummond on bass alongside Rufus Thibodeaux on fiddle, Ann Hilary O'Brien provided the obligatory harmony vocals and on one track, ex-Band member Levon Helm played drums. However the minimalist C&W backing suited the album's themes and preoccupations – there were, as ever, still plenty of Young's myopic obsessions with his own predicament, but he was able to look beyond them and survey the state of the Union, his own relationship to his adopted country and his position within it.

The mainly acoustic first side characteristically delved back into his ever-expanding catalogue of unreleased songs to provide two of the album's most absorbing cuts, 'Captain Kennedy' from the embryonic 'American Stars'n'Bars' and 'The Old Homestead', a song written with the 'Homegrown' project in mind. 'Kennedy', performed as a mock sea shanty, is thematically similar to another early contender for 'Stars'n'Bars', 'Powderfinger'. Whereas on the latter Young had assumed the role of the hapless teenager caught up in the throes of war, this time around he narrated the story in the third person and the young man here had the luxury of reflecting on the war to come and whether he was actually capable of killing his fellow human beings.

'Homestead' was immediately hailed by the train-spotter fans among Young's audience as another allegorical piece on his volatile relationship with Messrs Crosby, Stills & Nash. Each verse in the song is given over to a particular voice – the Shadow, the Rider and the three Birds for which some have

substituted manager Elliot Roberts (the Shadow), Young himself (the Rider – 'Why do you ride that Crazy Horse?') and CS&N (the three Birds – 'ditch this rider, shadow and all'). But if the song's intention was truly to comment on his ups and downs with CS&N, why should Young release it seven years later and at a time when another reunion would offer him scant artistic reward?

Reviewing it for *New Musical Express*, Cynthia Rose commented: 'out front sits Young . . . staring off into the Polaroid wilderness . . . and dreams dreams both personal and solid, visions that, ever since "Broken Arrow" are much like those of the First North American . . . the Indian (whose complex iconographies of the moon, the bird and the shadow-self weave a novel, mystic optimism on "The Old Homestead").'

After Ben began to make progress, Neil and Pegi embarked on a less strenuous programme of treatment for their son which allowed Young to return to the concert arena full-time

Side two was more uptempo, thigh-slapping hoedown music and more political to boot. Yet two songs 'Stayin' Power' ('Staying power through thick and thin') and 'Coastline' ('We don't back down from no trouble, we do get up in the mornin') were snapshots of the Youngs family's private life, and was a reflection of the dedication that had infused Neil and Pegi's life to provide their son with the immense amounts of love he needed.

'Comin' Apart At Every Nail' was Young lamenting the lot of the working man trying to scratch a living in the complex socio-economic climate of the late 20th Century, but it lacked the weight of, say, Woody Guthrie's stirring odes on the same subject. Nevertheless, the title cut gave a clear indication of Young's future alliances on the very eve of the presidential elections which would usher in the Reagan era, with its God-bless-America, be-thankful-for-what-we got sentiments. And, while Young knew that his adopted homeland and its history was far from unblemished, he still harboured a strong feeling of patriotism for the USA that would carry over into many of his views on life in the new decade.

Reaction

The Youngs' intense domestic situation up at the Broken Arrow ranch meant that there was to be no promotional tour for the new record. The next 18 months saw Young assisting Ben through his programme with typical single-mindedness. The main room in the ranch-house was converted, with areas of floor cleared for the boy to do his crawling exercises and other equipment in place for him to learn the use of his limbs. The program needed round-the-clock participation – initially from just Neil and Pegi and then, as the going got tougher, other members of the family and a team of volunteers would relieve them, contributing a morning here, an afternoon there.

Such dedication was bound to have a swinging kickback on his creative pursuits. The nature of his involvement in Ben's program meant that for the first time in his adult life, he was unable to please himself – take off to Santa Cruz, drive down to Nashville – and more importantly, music could no longer take centre stage as the be-all and end-all of his existence. He must, therefore, have treasured the moments of respite when he could slip away for a few hours into his home studio and pour these experiences into new material, as he explained to his father, Scott Young:

'You know, the songs I'm writing during the programme we're doing with Ben indicate to me how much what I'm doing every day is the strongest single influence on my work. The program with Ben is driving, implacable, repetitive, very strong, very strongly motivated. The music I've been writing in the last few months since the programme started is like that . . . driving, hopeful, repetitive.'

'Re.Ac.Tor', released in November 1981 (making Number 27 in the US, 69 in the UK), was the first of his albums ever to reach the master stage at his Broken Arrow Studio, all the selections being recorded without going off the ranch. Crazy Horse had been recalled as the sole backing musicians – and,

Neil Young in 1986, the US Cavalry hat badge and Indian-style beaded shirt a further reminder of his continuing homage to the mythic West of American history

Above: An unusual shot of Neil playing twelve-string guitar, which he featured only occasionally

Opposite: Neil in action during his visit to the United Kingdom that followed the release of 'Re.Ac.Tor', on stage at London's Wembley Arena in 1982

unlike so many earlier sets, the album featured a homogeneous collection of material. Yet given that Young had teamed up again with the dream team of Sampedro, Talbot and Molina, 'Re.Ac.Tor' was a bitter disappointment. Yes, its hard-rock grooves were 'repetitive', but hardly 'driving'.

It bristled with 'implacable', brutal and relentless guitar riffs that never quite permitted Young to take off on any of his exhilarating flights of lead guitar fancy, the grinding six-strings hammering out dense rhythms that created a heavy, industrial sound that seemed to go nowhere. And, for once, the listener was left with the thirst for some 'wooden' relief – a complaint that could never have been levelled at this classic line-up in the Seventies. Not even the presence of the full moon that Young cryptically needed during the sessions could lift the resultant music.

One track in particular, 'T-bone', epitomised this lurch towards what Adam Sweeting in *Melody Maker* described as 'a leaden morass of sound'. Young recalled its simple genesis: 'We were just in the studio and had already recorded the songs that we thought we were going to be recording. We still really felt like playing so I picked up my guitar and started playing. If you notice, the song starts with a straight cut right through the middle. We'd already started playing before the recording machine started. I just made up the lyrics and we did the whole thing that night. It was a one-take thing. It seems like the lyrics were just on my mind. It's very repetitive but I'm not such an inventive guy.'

For many, the instrumental excesses compounded the work's other major sin, his slide towards his identification with America's silent majority, that had begun to emerge on 'Hawks & Doves'. Young had long been obsessed with cars and the US automobile culture – he owns an extensive collection of classic vehicles – but 'Motor City', which could have been a celebration of the joys of four wheels, turned out to be a xenophobic rant on the erosion of America's traditional values and the United State's shrinking role in a changing world:

> *My old car keeps breaking down*
> *My new car ain't from Japan*
> *There's already too many Datsuns*
> *In this old town.*

This bigotry suggested that as the smoke cleared on the late Sixties/early Seventies, Young's followers had rather taken for granted his role in the peace'n'love vibes that CS&N embodied. Many of his songs from the early Eighties would see him clearly moving further and further away from the hallowed ideals of the Woodstock generation to which his former cohorts seemingly still clung.

Questioned at the time in *New Musical Express* about his relationship with his homeland and its role in his songwriting, Young was characteristically vague:

'North America's my home, I've been all over it. I don't write down all the things I see, I just watch until something comes out. Really I don't have a personal view on America as a whole. They're just disparate ideas that come together.'

Return to the Treadmill

The 'Re.Ac.Tor' sessions did, however produce a couple of gems: 'Southern Pacific', the single that reached a modest Number 70, saw Young back in a more comfortable area, exploring his own mythic America in the story of a forgotten, retired old rail worker. With the taming of the frontier, the American railways had been eclipsed in the 20th Century by the automobile, but railroad culture had a special place in his heart, even more so than his love of cars. Scott Young described the joys his son's huge model railway sets brought to Neil during this period:

'The train barn had been called the the car barn when I first visited in 1976 . . . now the cars had been moved to a San Francisco warehouse and the trains dominated the building. As some men can forget about everything while hunting or fishing . . . Neil's relaxation therapy is the trains.'

'Shots', first performed acoustically in New York in 1978, was the album's closer, now re-activated in burning electric form. The bad-tempered guitars echoed the morass of Young's confused feelings as he once again stared into the very heart of darkness and tried to reach some moral perspective on civilisation's apparent despair and decay.

Left: Keeping the music alive.

Right: Accepting the Hall of Fame award in Toronto in 1982, an acknowledgement of over fifteen years at the cutting edge of musical creativity

'Re.Ac.Tor' was also notable as being his last album for Reprise, at least for a while – he and Frank Sinatra were now the only remaining artists on the label. Sales on this latest waxing were among the worst of his career and he decided to switch to the AOR-dominated Geffen label. Yet despite millions of dollars that must have changed hands, it was to become a disastrous pairing.

On a positive note, the movie, *Human Highway*, long in the pipeline, was completed in early 1982, though in a different form to how it had been envisaged back in 1978. Actor Russ Tamblyn had subsequently joined the cast, while Dean Stockwell and Devo were retained from the original. Described as 'a comedy about a tragedy', it cast Young in the central role

of Lionel Switch, a none-too-bright worker at some futuristic nuclear plant. The narrative gradually built to the predictable atomic meltdown, following Switch en route through a long sequence in which he was hit on the head by an auto part and dreamed of being a rock star. Outside of his friends, family and camp followers, the movie met with a cool reaction, eliciting such a critical drubbing in the US trade weekly *Variety* that it found no distributor and met with a similar fate to its cine predecessor, *Journey Through The Past*.

This same period also saw an upturn in Young's domestic situation that was to have liberating and beneficial effects. Some definite progress had been made with Ben – as the boy's grandmother Margaret Morton observed:

'Until the program started, he was such a sad little boy. But when the program started and he had work to do every day, with the intense concentration of so many people around him trying to help, he just blossomed.'

However both Neil and Pegi were soon to be influenced by a seminar given by the National Academy of Child Development that advocated a less strenuous, less physical programme. This seemed much more appropriate for Ben's needs and his parents made the momentous decision to follow it through. The resolution was also to signal Neil's full-time return to the rock'n'roll treadmill and the concert arena.

During these months Neil was to renew his friendship with an old pal he hadn't seen since Buffalo Springfield days. Bruce Palmer had spent the past 12 years living in a Sikh commune in Toronto, having given up pop music to concentrate on the sitar. He had been living off a modest income from Springfield record royalties – a gesture from Young and Steve Stills, who had generously reinstated them in the early Seventies, long after Palmer had asked the pair to buy out his share in a lump sum to pay off a drug fine!

Suddenly he had felt the magnetic pull of rock'n'roll again – an urge he put down to 'boredom' – and had floated the idea of

a Buffalo Springfield reunion to the superstars. In a typical fit of loyalty, a trait Young has consistently displayed towards other musicians with whom he has enjoyed playing over the years, Neil consented to the idea and Palmer moved back to Los Angeles in anticipation of the planned reformation with all the original members (which was to include Dewey Martin and Richie Furay).

Catalyst

Stills' own hellish schedule killed off any chance of a reunion, but when Neil was putting together the nucleus of a band for an autumn tour of Europe, Palmer was invited out to Hawaii to join the rehearsals and recording sessions. It must have been a truly nerve-wracking experience for the bass player to suddenly find himself back in such exalted circles as he would later recall:

'I walk into this room with all those world-class musicians – Neil, Ralph Molina on drums, Ben Keith on pedal steel and keyboards, Nils Lofgren on guitar and keyboards and Joe Lala on percussion and vocals – and we start playing and I'm doing it as if I'd never been away!'

On returning to the mainland in June, Bruce Palmer was temporarily dropped – in a situation that echoed that of Danny Whitten a decade previously – on account of his personal 'habit', an over-reliance on alcohol. Physically he was now hardly recognisable as the skinny youth of the mid-Sixties, having filled out considerably over the years. Another bassist was sought and it looked like Bob Mosley might be recalled from exile, joining the outfit for a few weeks including a return gig at the Catalyst in Santa Cruz. The combination failed to click, however, and Young was back on the phone to Palmer: 'I

Displaying his characteristic loyalty to former fellow musicians, Young set out for Hawaii to rehearse and record with Bruce Palmer, Ralph Molina, Ben Keith and Nils Lofgren

Above: Nils Lofgren on stage with Young in 1982 during a series of concerts which witnessed Young's increasing interest in computer technology in music.

Opposite: When schedules allow – Young and Stills get together

need you, but only on condition that you control your drinking.' Palmer duly complied and on 31 August found himself on stage at the Parc de Sport in Annecy, France on the opening night of a series of European concerts that heralded Neil's first tour in four years. Playing 39 shows in nine countries, this return to the boards saw Young enjoying himself on a long walkway that extended from the centre of the stage right out into the audience. The European fans were treated to the new sight of their hero benefiting from the freedom of the radio microphone he'd first experimented with at the Bottom Line club in 1978. Drawing on his vast repertoire but with nothing from the last two albums, the concerts marked his first major use of computer technology and vocoders (that computerised voices) with which he had been experimenting for some time back at the ranch.

Electro-Pop

The singer had become a fan of German synth supremos Kraftwerk, and as a result had now begun his own forays into electro-pop. The tour debuted much of the material that would comprise 'Trans', his first LP for Geffen Records released in January 1983. This latest work was a complete departure for Young, but one about which he was both enthusiastic and proud. When the tour hit England for dates in Birmingham and London, Young was waxing lyrical about this new-found spirit of adventure:

'I spend most of my time trying to remain open to new things. They reflect the fact that I've got so interested in electronics and machines. I've always loved machines. I feel that with all the new digital and computerised equipment I can get my hands on now, I can do things I could never do before . . . I know this is just the beginning for me. I've been Neil Young for years and I could stay where I am and be a period piece but as I look around everything's so organised . . . the new music with its kind of perfection is reassuring for me . . . the manipulation of machines can be very soulful.'

This quest for a new voice and direction was greeted with general critical approval and the public bought it in sufficiently healthy numbers for it to reach Number 19 in America, 29 in the UK. 'Trans' was another of Neil Young's concept albums. It had its genesis in 'Island In The Sun', another recording project that had actually reached the test-pressing stage as Young would later divulge:

'It was the first record I made for Geffen. The three acoustic songs on "Trans" are from it. But they advised me not to put it out. Because it was my first record for Geffen, I thought "Well, this is a fresh new thing. He's got some new ideas". It didn't register to me that I was being manipulated.'

While Young could be applauded for his refusal to sit still, 'Trans' somehow smacked of contrivance. The whole project had the same hollow ring to it that paralleled ex-Byrd Roger McGuinn's proposed electronic collaboration with Brian Eno. Synthesized electro-pop was the prevailing unit-shifting force in the early-Eighties' rock marketplace – 'Trans' suggested that it was a case of the tail wagging the dinosaur, as Young now liked to refer to himself.

In one respect, it was another example of the singer's inner frustrations being expressed artistically. Just as 'Tonight's The Night' had seen Young exorcising the demons of Bruce Berry and Danny Whitten, much of the material on 'Trans' was inspired by son Ben's predicament.

'I did that album for my son, Ben,' he would later explain to *Melody Maker*: 'He's a non-oral child. And the scene of "Trans" is a hospital where there are all these people, bionic people, machines and robots, half people, half machines. They all work in this hospital and they have this little baby and they're trying to teach the baby how to communicate . . . there's one guy (Tabulon), he's made out of stuff like that guy C3PO in *Star Wars*. He's all kinda brass-looking and his face is a computer key-pad so whenever anything happens that needs figuring out, he starts hitting himself in the face.

'There were all kindsa characters. I had these nurses that sang, they were like clones of the Supremes. And, anyway, what they're all trying to do is make the baby communicate. That's what all the words are about. But you can't understand the words, because all the vocals are being put through vocoders and machines. That's the point I was making – how difficult and painful it can be to communicate, which is something we often just take for granted.'

Transformer

Young's experiments with drum machines, synths and vocoders dominated the record, from the blatant 'Sample And Hold' (a song that might have been more at home on the soundtrack to *Tron*) to the haunting 'Transformer Man' and 'Computer Cowboy' where the guitar riffs, which once reigned supreme, were disembodied by the prevailing chip technology. 'Mr Soul' received a similar refit, but a few more traditional tidbits were squeezed in among the technopop – 'Little Thing Called Love' (the album's single that got as far as Number 71 in the US) recalled the country honk of 'Stars'n'Bars', while 'Hold On To Your Love' found Young in romantic mood, though it was hardly the best of his love-sick ditties. 'Like An Inca' was another less than successful quest

for an Eighties 'Cortez' and caught him in a rare eco-minded moment, reflecting on the mind-blowing damage consistently being wrought upon the planet.

During the early Eighties, while many of his West Coast contemporaries were playing benefits for all manner of anti-nuclear and green concerns, Young came out on more than occasion in support of atomic power:

'We don't have it down, and we don't know what to do with the waste. But how are we going to get to the other planets? We need nuclear power to discover what's out there and discover another power source. A coal-burning rocket won't get there.'

Young has always been more socially than environmentally aware – a survey of all the benefit gigs he's ever played, would come out in favour of people (Native Americans, farmers, the handicapped, children, the Third World) rather than the natural world (compared with the preoccupations of, say, David Crosby) – and some of his best songs are informed by reverence for the man-made world, as much as they are by the redwood forests of his Northern Californian home.

With the release of the new album, Young went back to a heavy live schedule, promoting 'Trans' across the USA. He had parted company with the musicians used for the European jaunt which had marked the final collaboration with Nils Lofgren for a decade, the diminutive guitarist accepting the offer to reprise his role as first lieutenant and replace Miami Steve Van Zandt in the E Street Band. Instead Young would perform a solo, mostly acoustic show except for the finale – the 'Trans' section of the set where he enlisted backing from a dazzling array of computer technology.

To lighten the intermission, Neil indulged in a spot of fun and on a giant video-screen would appear the figure of Dan Clear (actor Newell Alexander), a wholesome, as American-as-apple-pie media personality who would announce information such as the location of the nearest fall-out shelter or give interviews with those backstage. It was decided to extend the tour by a further five weeks, but proceedings came to an abrupt halt on 4 March when the singer collapsed after the first set in Louisville, Kentucky. The illness which had been dogging him throughout the dates had finally laid him low, and the remaining shows were cancelled.

A few weeks' rest saw him sufficiently recovered and putting the finishing touches to a new collection of country songs entitled 'Old Ways'. This was not, however, destined to be the new album. According to Scott Young, the decision to delay the country material was down to Geffen Records:

'A couple of weeks later I asked Neil, "When is 'Old Ways' coming out?" He dragged out, "Well-l-l, it isn't right now. I got into writing some newer songs in the old Fifties rock style, a lotta fun. We recorded them and some others from that period and put that into an album. We had the record people up and played both 'Old Ways' and the newer one, 'Everybody's Rockin'', which is about as far removed from the 'Trans' kind of sound as it's possible to get. Anyway, we're putting out 'Everybody's Rockin'' first, 'Old Ways' will make it later."

This explanation euphemistically skated over the first in a series of rifts between the David Geffen Company and Young that would end with the label seeking $3 million in punitive and exemplary damages plus compensation from the artist in an LA Superior Court, the suit alleging that Young provided albums 'which were not commercial in nature and musically

Left: The tour brochure for 'Trans' offered a far lighter image than the music itself conveyed.

Right: On stage during the 'Trans' tour

characteristic of Young's previous records'. Talking later about the original 'Old Ways' recordings done in Nashville in mid-1983, Young told *Rolling Stone*'s James Henke:

'There was a whole other record, the original "Old Ways", which Geffen rejected. It was like "Harvest II"...I was so stoked about that record. I sent them a tape of it that had eight songs on it. I called them up a week later, cause I hadn't heard anything, and they said "Well frankly Neil, this record scares us a lot. We don't think this is the right direction for you to be going in." The techno pop thing was happening...I guess they just saw me as some old hippie from the Sixties still trying to make acoustic music or something; they looked at me as a product, and this didn't fit in with their marketing scheme.'

It's doubly mystifying, then, that the marketing execs at Geffen would pass up on a chance to release this return to the pastoral style of 'Harvest', Young's biggest-selling album, and issue the 25-minute 'Everybody's Rockin'', the back-to-the-roots rockabilly tribute, which they did in September 1983.

'Rockin'' is still regarded by Young as one of his favourite works, thematically placing it alongside 'Tonight's The Night' (and 1988's 'This Note's For You'), but the connection would have been missed by all but the most dedicated of his followers as they pored over its sleeve and espied the image of a bequiffed Neil, decked out in pink suit and matching tie, black shirt and two-tone shoes and strumming on a beautiful D'Angelico acoustic-bodied guitar. There was nothing particularly new or original about one of the rock establishment's most enduring stars tipping his hat to his Fifties roots – hadn't Lennon done it on 'Rock'n'Roll', Zappa & the Mothers on

Young opens his heart. No matter how many changes his music has gone through, Neil Young has carried a substantial hardcore of fans with him – enough to sustain him when hit singles have proved hard to find

'Ruben And The Jets' and Cooder on 'Bop Till You Drop'? What was so horrifying was that it should follow up the futuristic robo-rhythms of 'Trans'!

This time around Neil was backed by the Shocking Pinks – old faithful Ben Keith having ditched his pedal steel for a bopping alto sax, Tim Drummond plucking at an upright bass and drummer Karl Himmel keeping it all nice'n'simple on his snare. They're joined by a trio of doo-wop singers – Larry Byrom, Anthony Crawford and Rick Palombi, better known as the Redwood Boys. Perhaps taking a cue from the new breed of rootsy rockers like the Blasters crawling out of America's backwoods at the time, Young and company rocked up a storm on a set that was fat on cover versions, lean on originals. But that was no great loss, if throwaway floss like 'Kinda Fonda Wanda' is anything to go by.

Rockin' Pink

At times Young misread the non-original material: 'Mystery Train', as *Melody Maker* noted, 'completely misses the coiled distemper of a Presley or the spooky foreboding that the Band gave it' (ironically, Ben Keith had guested on the album, 'Moondog Matinee', which had boasted this version). But most of the time he and the other musicians sounded like they were having the time of their lives. Of Young's own songs, 'Rainin' In My Heart' worked as a beautiful rereading of some of Hank Williams's finest moments and, lurking underneath 'Payola Blues' (written as far back as 'Goldrush' days), was a stream of bile that ranked among Young's bitterest. Aimed at the jocks who won't play your record until big bucks have changed hands, it was dedicated to the 'father of rock'n'roll' – Alan Freed, the DJ who pioneered R&B radio back in the Fifties and who was later indicted on payola charges to die destitute in Palm Springs in 1965.

In May 1982, manager Elliot Roberts had commented that Young approached his art 'like a painter' his records were not

all destined to be commercial or the Mona Lisa, some would be smaller works and others important. A convenient interpretation of his protégé's highs and lows, maybe, but it could not conceal the fact that 'Rockin'' was an expensive indulgence for his beleaguered following and cold comfort for Geffen Records hoping to recoup their millions with an album that probably should have been a mini LP or 12" single.

The Harvesters

Young decided to stick with the Shocking Pinks and used them as his tour band – after an hour or so of more conventional fare, shows of this period would see the band return to the stage looking like a bunch of renegade Teds for a rumbustious finale of pure, unadulterated rock'n'roll. And then on some

Above: Jamming with country-and-western renegade Waylon Jennings in 1985, with whom Young would share vocals on many of the tracks on 'Old Ways'.

Opposite: In New York with the International Harvesters, 1985

occasions they'd be further augmented by girl singers, the Pinkettes, who'd feature Pegi Young when her busy schedule as a mother permitted.

His enthusiasm for rockabilly proved as short-lived as had his dalliance with computers on 'Trans'. February 1984 saw Young rehearsing with Crazy Horse once again and playing some gigs at his favourite watering hole in Santa Cruz, the Catalyst. But this latest return to the fold turned out badly and ensuing sessions, working on new songs like 'Violent Side' and 'Stand By Me' (with Billy Talbot replacing his boss on lead vocals) in Young's opinion 'sucked'! The ever-faithful Horse was sent back to the stable and Young set about assembling a new backing group out of the ashes of the Shocking Pinks. Adding fiddler Rufus Thibodeaux and keyboard player Spooner Oldham to the nucleus of Ben Keith, Tim Drummond, Anthony Crawford and Karl Himmel, Neil celebrated his rediscovered love of the bucolic life and christened the outfit the International Harvesters.

The dispute with Geffen worsened, with the company digging in over its refusal to issue a fully-blown Country and Western album. Young became equally entrenched and the lawsuits began to fly thick and fast. It would be up to another two years before the successor to 'Everybody's Rockin'' would appear. But even if Geffen weren't prepared to release a country album, it wasn't going to stop the singer writing and performing material in that vein. The negative feelings had reached an absolute frenzy, as Young would later recall in *Q* magazine:

'...I told them the longer you sue me for playing country music, the longer I'm going to play country music. Either you back off or I'm going to play country music forever. And you won't be able to sue me anymore because country music will be what I always do so it won't be uncharacteristic anymore, hahaha. So stop telling me what to do or I'll turn into George Jones.'

And if his descent into an unbending pursuance of pure cornball C&W wasn't enough, Young appeared to embrace many of its redneck, right-wing morals – total anathema to his more hip fans whose own ideals were taking a pasting in the early Eighties from Reagan and Thatcher's free-market economy, autocratic style of government and their unflinching belief in the continuance of a massive Western arms build-up. Young could perhaps have been forgiven for praising Reagan's call to return to family values, given his own situation and the importance that the family holds in the broad sweep of maudlin country and western music. By now he was regularly performing a new tune, 'Nothing Is Perfect', that reflected this absorption with family ties. In retrospect, he would observe:

'I became much more involved in family, taking care of the family, making sure the family was secure. And I related to Reagan's concept of big government and federal programs fading away so that communities could handle their own programs, like day care. That was the crux of his domestic message, and I thought the idea was good. I thought it would bring people together. But it was a real idealistic thing, and people didn't really come together.'

But his public support for Reagan's aggressive overseas policies was far harder to swallow. Speaking in *Melody Maker* in 1985, Young was in loquacious if somewhat confused mood. Grilled by Adam Sweeting about his enthusiasm for America's role in the escalation of the arms race, Young remarked:

'Ten years ago the US was starting to really drag ass, way behind the Soviets in build-up. All that's happened lately is more or less to catch up, just to be equal, reach equality in arms. At best it's a bad situation, but I think it would be worse to be weak when the stronger nation is the aggressor against freedom. So I stand behind Reagan when it comes to build-up, to stand, be able to play hardball with other countries that are aggressive towards free countries. I don't think there's anything wrong with that.'

In the same interview he admitted that he wouldn't have felt that way in 1967 but he was 'an older man now' with a family and that, while there was no immediate threat to his own, he could identify with the threat to families on the borders of the Iron Curtain. Asked about the mind-boggling cost of maintaining a nuclear arsenal, he agreed that it was 'crazy...fucking nuts', but countered:

'At least in our countries we have the fucking freedom to stand up and say it's crazy. And that's what we're fighting for,

to be able to disagree. Openly . . . So I don't put down anybody who says we should stop building weapons . . . idealistically I agree with them. It's like walking both sides of the fence – but I think there's too much to be responsible for as men and as people, that you actually have to take care of your own.'

When Sweeting picked Young up on this last remark as reeking of an 'every man for himself' selfishness, it seemed to call his bluff and Young could only bluster:

The International Harvesters: it was unclear whether Young's wholesale embrace of C&W was to annoy his record company or an attempt to 'burn out' in the face of his 40th birthday . . .

'Sort of, but . . . I think it's more like every man for his brother than every man for himself.'

It wasn't difficult to see where this influence was emanating from: Young had surrounded himself with country musicians and the band was playing venues far removed from rock'n'roll arenas – state fairs and carnivals, day-long gatherings of audiences made up from several generations – that only served to reinforce his cherished ideal of the family. That was part of the attraction of playing C&W music, too, as he remarked to *Melody Maker*: 'I see country music, I see people who take care of their own. You got 75 year old guys on the road. That's what I was put here to do, y'know, so I wanna make sure I surround myself with people who are gonna take care of me. Cos I'm in it for the long run.'

This last remark had an ominous ring to it. Was his new love affair with country music his way of sidetracking from his cherished notion that it was 'better to burn out than to fade away'? Staring the big 4-oh in the face, was Young ready to abandon rock?

'It really doesn't leave you a way to grow old gracefully and continue to work . . . rock'n'roll is young people's music . . . I still love rock'n'roll, but I don't see a future there for me.'

Hayseed and Sawdust

He continued to work and tour extensively with the International Harvesters, who by this time had developed into a highly proficient unit that added just the right amount of hayseed and sawdust to his new country tunes and a new raw dimension to the older more traditional fare such as 'Southern Pacific' which rolled along like a well-oiled caboose in their hands. They would even slip in the occasional surprise choice such as a revamp of the old Buffalo Springfield chestnut, 'Flying On The Ground Is Wrong', while 'Down By The River' from 'Everybody Knows This Is Nowhere' was still being delivered with a fearsome hard-rock edge.

1985 was a confusing year with Young batting from all sides: he was right behind Reagan's arms build-up but still in line with the various aids benefits of the era

In 1984 Young had publicly stated in a radio interview that he would never agree to another reunion with CS&N, until David Crosby kicked his far-gone addiction to freebase cocaine. So it was a pleasant surprise to fans all over the world when, in addition to a set with the Harvesters, Young joined his mates on stage at Live Aid on 15 July 1985 for a one-off reformation (Crosby was out of jail on an appeal bond). About the reunion, he told *Melody Maker*:

'David says that he loves to play music with CSN&Y more than anything in the world. I told them when they could prove

to me that that's really what he wanted to do with his life and give up drugs, that I would go out with them . . . Live Aid was an exception to the rule. I will not go out with CSN&Y, have everyone scrutinise the band, how big it is and how much it meant, and see this guy that's so fucked up on drugs, and who's really not so fucked up that he can't come back because we've all seen him when he's been clean recently, where he's very sharp just like he always was...'

Farm Aid

Taking it's cue from Live Aid, Neil was caught up in a Canadian equivalent of Band Aid and sang on a single, 'Tears Are Not Enough' under the guise of Northern Lights with a host of other name rockers including Bryan Adams, ex-Hawks Ronnie Hawkins and singer Joni Mitchell. Maybe the irony that all the billions the West was spending on weapons could have been used to feed the world just passed him by!

However Young was soon to be taking part in another act of charity that was both nearer home and closer to his heart. Farm Aid saw stars from both the rock and country worlds come together for what would turn out be an ongoing series of benefit gigs for America's small farmers. Young became one of the prime movers behind this organization and, on 22 September, he duly appeared onstage at the University of Illinois' football stadium in the company of Willie Nelson, Joni Mitchell, Bob Dylan, Johnny Cash and a crowd of other

Live Aid: honoured not only with a set from the Harvesters but also CSN&Y, despite Young's avowal not to play with Crosby again until the latter had overcome his drug addiction

celebrities. The concert raised over $10 million which was spent on legal aid for those facing loan foreclosures on their farms and on psychiatric counselling (the suicide rate in the farming community was becoming an increasing problem).

At the same time Geffen finally relented and agreed to release another Young album. Though entitled 'Old Ways', this was in fact a new set superseding the 1983 recordings that had been rejected out of hand. The Harvesters were augmented for this recording by a who's who of heavyweight Nashville talent including Hargus 'Pig' Robbins and Ralph Mooney. Particularly intriguing was the way in which Young chose to share vocals on almost every track with another male lead voice, supplied either by Willie Nelson or Waylon Jennings, the notorious outlaws of modern country and western.

Superficially, 'Old Ways' recalled the winsome delights of the 'Comes A Time' album and even reunited its maker with some of the Gone With The Wind Orchestra, whose swelling strings had made that particular album so memorable. Indeed the strings add a similar feel, a blast of sweet prairie air on the opening 'Wayward Wind', a tune popularised by Tex Ritter. But 'Old Ways' was straight-laced, dyed-in-the-wool contemporary country, awash with a cloying sentimentality that rendered the likes of 'Once An Angel' and what appeared to be Young's anthem 'Get Ready For The Country' almost unlistenable to an audience more used to his abrasive rock settings – even if, in Nashville circles, it must have been something of an event. 'My Boy' was even worse, little more than a sickly hickory reworking of the old Cat Stevens song 'Father And Son'.

One of the record's more intelligent cuts, 'Are There Any More Real Cowboys?', was the basis of a video promo starring Willie Nelson. This hymn to the ways of the traditional cattle wrangler was underscored with an attack on government-backed, modern farming methods that were causing the very disappearance of the mythical 'Marlboro man'. One tune stood out amid all the redneck sentiments like an oasis in the desert, and represented Young at his most potent. Starting out like a country retake of Bowie's 'Space Oddity', 'Misfits' saw Young treading the same ground as he had on 'Shots' – an eerie and bleak song that mused on alienation, 'an anthem for the lost' with sweeping strings that rendered it a beautiful, disturbing epic. As *Broken Arrow* magazine commented: 'the irony is that Waylon and Willie listeners may well skip the non-country 'Misfits' at the end of the first side, flip it over and miss a whole dimension of Neil.' It was the one genuinely transcending moment on the album, proving that even at his most conservative and basic, Young could still write songs both humane and surreally provocative.

Although Geffen softened enough to release 'Old Ways', a subsequently recorded five-track EP that ploughed the same country vein (including 'Depression Blues' and 'Interstate') to raise funds for Farm Aid was nixed. It was to be Young's final collaboration with the International Harvesters.

Neil's family life continued to take centre-stage during this period. On 15 May his third child Amber Jean was born, a healthy little girl 'just a little flower, growing like a little flower should' he would later comment. And he and his wife embarked on a new and important project for son Ben, the setting up of the Bridge School to be run by Pegi and for which

The Farm Aid concert in September 1985 was the first in a series of such benefit gigs that Young and his cohorts would play – after the bucolic aspirations of his youth, the plight of the farmers was of particular importance to him

Young was to organise annual fund-raising events and other forms of sponsorship. The first benefit gig in November 1986 saw Don Henley, Tom Petty, Bruce Springsteen, and Robin Williams join Crosby Stills Nash & Young at the Shoreline Amphitheatre in Mountain View, California before 17,000 fans.

Landing on Water

As Young's career began to stumble along its wayward path in the early Eighties, fans of his of work with the Springfield and Crazy Horse could take shelter in the proliferation of young new bands that were exploding across America at the time, many of which acknowledged a debt to the Loner. Jason and the Scorchers branded 'Are You Ready For The Country' their own, while Green On Red's 1985 breakthrough album, 'Gas, Food & Lodging' overflowed with the sizzling firepower of 'Zuma', their leader Danny Stuart quipping 'if you're gonna steal, steal the best!'

Indeed there's an apocryphal tale that relates to this album, wherein DJ Andy Kershaw in an interview played Green On Red's 'Sea Of Cortez'. It caused Neil to respond, 'that's Crazy Horse!' The Beat Farmers, the Dream Syndicate and many others tipped their cowboy hats at Neil's illustrious past – none more so than LA's fabulous Rain Parade, early incarnations of which moved critics to compare them with the Springfield, while later line-ups publicly proclaimed 'Crazy Horse as godhead'!

It's unlikely, however, that these combos were the reason behind Young's sudden return to playing rock in the summer of 1986 with 'Landing On Water'. 'That album was like a rebirth,' he'd later tell *Rolling Stone*, 'just me coming back to LA after having been secluded for so long. I was finding my rock'n'roll roots again. And my vibrancy as a musician. Something came alive; it was like a bear waking up.' The guitarist did not, however, call up Crazy Horse, his old standbys for occasions such as this. Instead he holed up at Record One Studios in Los Angeles and recorded the whole affair with Steve Jordan on drums and Danny Kortchmar on guitars, with all three of them handling synthesizer chores. Kortchmar, best known for his work with James Taylor and soft rockers the Section, was an unusual choice, though he was later feted for providing the impetus on Rolling Stone Keith Richards' solo debut 'Talk is Cheap' (on which Jordan also appeared and co-produced).

'Landing On Water' was in a sense Young's olive branch to Geffen, its synthesizer-dominated tracks suggesting that this

Session singer Nicolette Larson joining Young and the

International Harvesters on stage during a performance at

Pier 84 in New York in 1985

time around, Neil was prepared to conform and hitch his horse to the prevailing styles of mid-Eighties adult-oriented rock that were selling by the bucketload for his new record label. Jordan's drums were consistently to the fore, giving cuts like 'Weight Of The World' a late-period Police flavour, but most of the record was unbearably cluttered with whining guitars and flaccid riffs that went off at half-cock. 'Landing' suffered from a sterile, compressed sound that not even Neil's voice or ear

Opposite: ' . . . the excesses of our whole generation. From hippie to yuppie – it's been quite an evolution.' Young back on stage with Crosby and Nash in 1986.

Below: Backstage preparations

for melody could save from disaster. And it boasted one of the worst sleeves in the history of rock, the crashing aeroplanes ironically echoing the nosedive Young's career would take with this album. In short, on this album Neil looked like he was totally lost at sea.

Predictably it got a unanimous thumbs-down from critics. 'Nothing about "Landing On Water",' sighed Adam Sweeting in *Melody Maker*, 'suggests confidence, creativity or conviction', while *New Musical Express* dismissed it as 'the same old drivel'. Lyrically the new set gave little relief, either, although it did include 'Hippie Dream' – a broadside aimed at David Crosby, now at the very nadir of his drug habit. Young was in no mood to mince words. 'The tie-dye sails are the screamin'

sheets,' he spat. 'The wooden ships are a hippie dream cap-sized in excess.' Young might not have been at the end of his tether like he was on 'Ambulance Blues' but for him Crosby's drug hell symbolised the end of the line for all those once lofty and cherished Sixties' aspirations. Discussing the song in *Rolling Stone*, he commented:

'I wrote that for Crosby. But I guess it could have been for me, or anybody. It's really about the excesses of our whole generation. From hippie to yuppie – it's been quite an evolution.'

Honeymoon

Young's planned summer 1986 tour of Europe was cancelled – and without the stimulus of live promotion, 'Landing On Water' would only reach Number 52 in the UK charts, his worst showing since 'Re.Ac.Tor'. In the States, it peaked six places higher but nothing since 'Trans' had breached the US Top 40. With his commercial standing at rock bottom, there was nothing else for it but to round up Crazy Horse.

'One morning I woke up and all I could hear was this massive fucking beat. And my guitar was just rising out of it. I just heard rock'n'roll in my head, so fucking loud that I couldn't ignore it.' The quartet set out on a tour of the north-eastern states – the 'Rusted Out Garage Tour' – their first together since 1978. And thematically it continued some of that era's traditions, employing more outsize props – this time a lawn mower, a spider and a mechanical cockroach! It was hard to believe that the man who, only months before, had been threatening to give up rock in favour of C&W was up there on stage again tearing shrieking feedback and all other manner of distortion from his instrument. Neil Young the manic rock'n'roll animal was back!

But it was to be a short honeymoon period – the tour was a dazzling return to form for both the guitar hero and Crazy Horse, now describing themselves as 'the third-best garage band in the world'. (They never alluded as to who was better!)

Work began on a new album – fans held their breath. If anyone could bring the best out in the maestro, it was Messrs Molina, Talbot and Sampedro. In spring 1987 European audiences had the chance to find out whether there was a real foundation to the rumours of this rebirth. They were to be severely disappointed. By the time Crazy Horse reached the UK they seemed to be flagging – the high-energy ferocity that had long fuelled Young and Sampedro's guitar duels was in danger of drying up.

Young had a lot of ground to make up with his overseas fans, mystified and depressed by his subsequent chameleon-like changes of musical direction since the European shows of 1982, during which segments of the audience had openly booed the 'Trans' material. The tour with Crazy Horse did little to restore their faith. Ticket sales were so bad that the party was stranded in France for four days when some shows were cancelled – not surprisingly morale in the band was extremely low and relations strained. And Young would later attest that he had actually documented his band while it was coming apart at the seams on a home movie which he had shot while they were on the road in Europe, and which he referred to as *Muddy Track*:

'I had two little Video-8 cameras, which I left running all the time. I would just come into rooms and put them down on the table. And the point of view is really from the camera. The camera takes on an identity – its name is Otto – and people start talking to the camera. And this camera saw a lot of things that really go down on a tour that are not cute or funsywunsy. It's not like the pop-band-on-the-road type of thing. There's a lot of guts in it, a lot of feeling . . . there's some wild stuff in there where we do speed metal. A lot of the music is only the beginnings and ends of songs. The songs aren't there. It's like the interviews are only the interviewer. And you hardly ever see me. You only hear questions. It's an interesting concept of your point of view...'

The band returned to California – was this the end of a beautiful relationship? Later, in *Rolling Stone* magazine, Neil seemed to think the marriage was over:

'The question is, how long can you keep doing it? And really be doing it? Or do you just become a re-enactment of an earlier happening? Toward the end, it was starting to. I could feel it starting to slip away. And I never ever wanted to be in front of people and have them pay to see me when I'm not 100 per cent there...I may come back to Crazy Horse again some day, but it seems unlikely.'

The new recordings with Crazy Horse were released as 'Life' the following summer – and, while it represented a step forward from the synthetic lows of 'Landing', the record failed to capitalise on the raw energy that crackled when the band had reconvened the previous autumn. The 'garage-rock' tracks like 'Too Lonely' failed to ignite, while 'Cryin' Eyes' was a pale imitation of the work-out the Ducks had given it. Connoisseurs of real 'garage rock' laughed at the clichéd 'Prisoners Of Rock'n'Roll' – which, even if it was intended to be tongue in cheek, only an ageing rocker could have written – and dove into their pile of Celibate Rifles or Sonic Youth records for a blast of the real McCoy! Crazy Horse were, for the most part, just too sloppy to bring home the bacon and Neil seemed sadly incapable of reining in his love of chip technology to let their natural creative juices flow.

Even long-time admirer and *Melody Maker* editor Allan Jones was plainly ready to give up the ghost with Young after hearing 'Life', consigning it to the great rock'n'roll dumper in a river of journalistic vitriol. 'This rag-bag of ill-tempered patriotic posturing and menopausal raunch,' Jones wrote, 'is final proof that the once great man has completely lost the plot.' Yet for all of Jones' anger, parts of 'Life' do bear up to close scrutiny. 'Inca Queen' was further exploration of his obsession with the primitive cultures of Central America – weaving in another of his favourite themes, the concept of time travel which had made some of the songs on 'Rust' so intriguing. The song was characterised by some beautiful guitar passages which perfectly enhanced its Spanish flavour.

'Mideast Vacation' was a pile-driver with Neil reconsidering his earlier gung-ho endorsement of America's expansionist overseas policies. This and the slower 'Long Walk Home' (a reflection on the self-inflicted wounds America had suffered from involvement in Vietnam and Beirut) saw the singer and writer gradually arriving at the realisation that nothing on the

In 1986, after a break of around eight years, Neil and Crazy Horse teamed up once more to tour and record an album – it was a dazzling but short-lived return to form

world stage was quite as clear-cut or as black and white as he would have had us believe when he saw life through the eyes of an Okie.

'Life' also found Young in better voice than he had been in for a long time, no more so than on the mysterious 'We Never Danced'. This closing number, one of the album's few real highlights, reunited the singer with Jack Nitzsche, whose arrangement and plangent piano accompaniment contributed so much to its enigmatic and ghostly charm. For once, Young

signed off a new album on a musical high, even if its chart positions of US 75/UK 71 were disappointing.

Crazy Horse may have been put out to grass but Young was as busy as ever, immersing himself in all kinds of different activities. In June he returned to Winnipeg for a reunion with the Squires, his first professional band, this being filmed for Canadian television. On 19 September he performed at Farm Aid II at the University of Nebraska's Memorial Stadium with John Cougar Mellencamp, Joe Walsh, Lou Reed and others. Young chose the show to debut a spanking new band – the Blue Notes, assembled from the ashes of Crazy Horse.

Just prior to his final acrimonious divorce from them earlier in the year, they'd done some American dates together:

'When we came home from the tour of Europe last summer we did a small tour of the States where I did an acoustic show to start with. Then I did a little set of blues material with one of the roadies playing sax and Poncho from Crazy Horse on organ. We set it up like a little lounge kind of thing. We would take an intermission, then Crazy Horse would do a "Crazy Horse" set, which by that time was not much of a challenge. It wasn't turning me on too much. So when I listened back to the tapes that we had recorded, I found myself only listening back to the three or four blues-type songs. That was all I liked. I enjoyed it and it sounded good. Then we enhanced the group by adding five more horns, and then we changed the bass and drums. That's the way the Blue Notes is.'

Young was now referring to himself as Shakey Deal and joining him were Frank 'Poncho' Sampedro on keyboards, Rick 'The Bass Player' Rosas, drummer Chad Cromwell, Ben Keith on steel guitar and alto saxophone and the mighty horns of Steve Lawrence (tenor sax), Claude Caillet (trombone), John Fumo (trumpet), Larry Cragg (baritone sax) and Tom Bray (trumpet). He'd even tried out his old Buffalo Springfield pals Dewey Martin and Bruce Palmer as a possible rhythm section. Skulking behind this latest mask, Young was now a born-again bluesman, the Blue Notes belting out an irresistible brew of high-powered rhythm'n'blues. The singer was nothing less than ecstatic about this latest aggregation, enthusing to *Rolling Stone*:

'Right now I love the Blue Notes, to a point where it feels so right to me. I think it's the best support I've had for the kind of music I was into. Everything has come together at the right time for this. There's a special thing that happens when the music is right. When it's not hard to do. When things aren't a problem. And you just play, and everybody likes it, and they start grooving. That makes me write a new song every morning when I wake up, instead of thinking "Well, if I write this, are the guys gonna be able to play it, or have I got the right band, or do I know anybody who really understands who I am, who I can actually play music with?"'

Renaissance

His old enthusiasm had returned, and the satisfaction with his current musical direction was given a further boost on 7 October 1987 when manager Elliot Roberts called to say that it finally looked as if Neil was about to break free of Geffen's artistic straitjacket and leave the label. It must have been one of the most exhilarating moments of his life. Looking back on his time with Geffen, he mused:

'It's hard for me to disassociate the frustrations that I had during that period from the actual works I was able to create. I really tried to do my best during that period, but I felt that I was working under duress . . . they had a very negative viewpoint of anything that I wanted to do, other than straight pop records that were exactly what they wanted to hear. They saw me as a product that was not living up to their expectations. They didn't see me as an artist . . . in all my time at Warner Brothers, they never once cancelled a session. Not for any reason. And it happened several times at Geffen. It was just blatant manipulation. It was just so different from anything I'd experienced . . . they buried "Everybody's Rockin'". They did less than nothing. They decided, "That record's not gonna get noticed. We're gonna press as few of those as possible and not do anything."'

The Crazy Horse quartet of Young, Frank Sampredo, Billy Talbot and Ralph Molina reached Europe in the spring of 1987 where fans were waiting to see if 'the third-best garage band in the world' – as they were wont to call themselves – were really back on form. Unfortunately, the initial promise of greatness had deserted them and fans were bitterly disappointed

But his troubles with Geffen had not only stemmed from his inability to cope with their corporate inflexibility. At the root of his artful contrariness nagged more personal worries, and it was these problems that ultimately informed his creative output during this era:

'It's a subtle thing, but it's right there. But it has to do with a part of my life that practically no-one can relate to. So my music, which is a reflection of my inner self, became something that nobody could relate to. And then I started hiding in styles, just putting little clues in there as to what was really on my mind. I just didn't want to openly share all this stuff in songs that said exactly what I wanted to say in a voice so loud everyone could hear it.'

On his departure from Geffen, one of Young's most urgent plans was to release a three-record set, 'Decade II' which would put his recent genre-hopping activities for that label into perspective and hopefully balance the books for his bemused public. 'Decade II' was a project that Geffen, with its overriding commercial interests, would never have allowed Young to pursue. Sadly, the project was to be superseded by plans to release an even more ambitious anthology timed to celebrate his 25th anniversary as a rock artist . . . scheduled for 1992 but still in the pipeline two years later.

With a return to his beloved Reprise Records imminent and a new album of upbeat, accessible blues tunes in the pipeline, life at the end of 1987 looked undeniably rosy. Young could also enjoy the first major success from his record production company the Volume Dealers, which he'd set up with Nick Bolas, with the acclaimed Warren Zevon set 'Sentimental Hygiene'. Zevon was on top form, no doubt inspired by the album's backing musicians which included most of REM, Bob Dylan and Young himself. The album's title track was alight with the Loner's crackling lead guitar lines – he'd never sounded fitter. Clearly, the wilderness years for Neil Young were finally drawing to a close.

'Hawks'n'Doves' (1980)

After the electric onslaught of 'Live Rust', Young chose to open the Eighties with this low-key collection, the first side of which was gentle and acoustic, the second more heartily country-flavoured.

'Comin' Apart At Every Nail' was a paean to the tough lot of the ordinary working man, while the title track had Young in a patriotic, flag-waving mood, a portent of the philosophy Young subsequently nurtured in the Eighties. Away from the politics, 'Hawks'n'Doves' ranged from the personal to the almost jokey. 'Coastline' and 'Stayin' Power' were reflections on his home life, while 'Union Man' sniped at the American Federation of Musicians. But the best moments, here, were the unpretetentious love song, 'Little Wing' (not the Hendrix number) and two from the Seventies – 'Captain Kennedy', a companion piece to 'Powder Finger' performed as a mock sea shanty and 'The Old Homestead', a dark, allegorical opus originally written for 1974's aborted 'Homegrown' set.

Track Listing:

Little Wing • The Old Homestead • Lost In Space • Captain Kennedy •
Stayin' Power • Coastline • Union Man • Comin' Apart At Every Nail •
Hawks'n'Doves

'Re.Ac.Tor' (1981)

With Crazy Horse back in harness, this should have heralded a return to the hard-rock heights of 'Rust Never Sleeps'. Sadly, it wallowed in a bog of impenetrable, crude guitar riffs that never managed to break free of the leaden rhythms which characterised most of the tracks. 'Re.Ac.Tor' was recorded in its entirety at Young's ranch, in the odd hours of respite his relentless domestic situation allowed him and it bristled with an inner torment that his performance here, especially on 'T-bone' and the long final cut, 'Shots', seemed unable to assuage.

'Motor City' marked his further slide towards identification with the silent majority – a frighteningly bigoted rant about America's inability to maintain its number one position in the world's economic pecking order. 'Southern Pacific' was one of the few gems, an ode to the halcyon days of the old railroads and the story of a retired and forgotten railroad man. It returned to the era of the frontier, to a simpler time about which Young obviously felt happier and more comfortable.

Track Listing:

Opera Star • Surfer Joe And Moe The Sleaze • T-bone • Get Back On It • Southerern Pacific • Motor City • Rapid Transit • Shots

'Trans' (1983)

Young's weirdest departure from the rock'n'roll straight and narrow, 'Trans' saw him experimenting with all manner of computer technology. Written for handicapped son Ben, the album is set in a futuristic hospital staffed by bionic people, who are teaching a small baby to communicate. On some tracks Young's heavily 'vocoded' vocals are almost unrecognisable, and the accompaniment a reflection that the singer nowadays felt as comfortable with electronic gadgets as he did with an acoustic guitar.

But in the midst of all the microchip technology lurked more traditional fare like 'Little Thing Called Love', a catchy country-rocker, 'Hold On To Your Love', a stab at the straight commercial pop of 'Harvset' and 'Like An Inca' which harked back to the 'Zuma' era. The backing included Buffalo Springfield bass player Bruce Palmer, most of Crazy Horse and Nils Lofgren, on his last collaboration with Neil for more than a decade.

Track Listing:

Little Thing Called Love • Computer Age • We R In Control • Transformer Man • Computer Cowboy (AKA Syscrusher) • Hold On To Your Love • Sample And Hold • Mr Soul • Like An Inca

'Everybody's Rockin'' (1983)

After the space-age 'Trans', nobody could have guessed that Neil would trade his microchips for a semi-acoustic and his vocoder for a quiff. Young was revisiting his Fifties roots and with a new band, the Shocking Pinks, whipping out a set of authentic doo-wop and rockabilly that bore comparison with both Lennon's 'Rock'n'Roll' and the Band's 'Moondog Matinee' albums.

The concept hinted that it would be a mere collection of cover versions, but infact Young had captured the flavour of the era by giving his own songs very Fifties titles ('Kinda Fonda Wanda', 'Rainin' In My Heart' etc). Of the four non-Young tunes, 'Betty Lou's Got A New Pair Of Shoes', penned by Bobby Freeman, was the most enjoyable and successful interpretation. Of the originals, 'Rainin'' – a Hank Williams-style pastiche and the vitriolic 'Payola Blues' (dedicated to the late Alan Freed) scored well.

Track Listing:

Betty Lou's Got A New Pair Of Shoes • Rainin' In My Heart • Payola Blues • Wonderin' • Kinda Fonda Wanda • Jellyroll Man • Bright Lights, Big City • Cry, Cry, Cry • Mystery Train • Everybody's Rockin'

'Old Ways' (1985)

Surrounding himself with dependable regulars like Ben Keith and Tim Drummond and some of Nashville's finest session men such as pedal steel guitarist Ralph Mooney and pianist Hargus 'Pig' Robbins, Young turned in a collection of country tunes that were quite as authentic as those on 'Everybody's Rockin'',and the whole project was given a seal of approval by the presence of the genre's most notorious outlaws, Willie Nelson and Waylon Jennings, on almost every track.

One of the standout cuts was the cover of Tex Ritter's 'The Wayward Wind', which reunited Neil with members of the Gone With the Wind Orchestra from 'Comes A Time'. Many selections such as the title track, the ironic 'Are There Any More Real Cowboys?' and 'Get Back To The Country' embodied Young's new-found love of the bucolic lifestyle, but 'Misfits' showed that, under the Okie disguise, there still lurked the perceptive, poetic mind of yore.

Track Listing:

The Wayward Wind • Get Back To The Country • Are There Any More Real Cowboys? • Once An Angel • Misfits • California Sunset • Old Ways • My Boy • Bound For Glory • Where Is The Highway Tonight?

'Landing On Water' (1986)

While Young could be applauded for keeping one step ahead of his audience with three wilfully diverse concept albums, there could be no such excuse for the AOR-dominated 'Landing On Water'.

Recording with just drummer Steve Jordan and guitarist Danny Kortchmar (best known for his work with James Taylor and Carole King), Young came up with a modern commercial album that managed to please neither his own fans nor the contemporary pop audience. Its percussive, keyboard-heavy muzak was positively inedible. Only the lyrics offered the beleaguered Young fan a glimmer of interest – notably on 'Hippie Dream', purportedly an open letter to David Crosby, then at the very depths of his drug habit – but it could equally be regarded as another meditation, as 'Ambulance Blues' had been, on the final crumbling of all those Sixties hopes and aspirations.

Track Listing:

Weight Of The World • Violent Side • Hippie Dream • Bad News Beat • Touch The Night • People On The Street • Hard Luck Stories • I Got A Problem • Pressure • Drifter

'Life' (1987)

This latest Crazy Horse collaboration was a pale imitation of the classic trails they'd blazed together in the Seventies. The return to a basic 'garage-rock' approach was a welcome antidote to the previous album's synthetic dross, but in the wake of Young's recent dramatic changes of direction a slew of young bands had reared their pimply little heads with fresh feisty rock that made Crazy Horse sound very middle-aged.

The only lesson that Neil seemed to have learnt was that the world was, after all, a far more complicated place than his redneck ideals had led him to believe. 'Mideast Vacation' and 'Long Walk Home' suggested that he was reconsidering the hawkish stance that he had once been so ready to adopt. Musically the one true highlight of 'Life' was the eerie, obscure 'We Never Danced', in which he teamed up again with Jack Nitzsche. On completion of this record, Neil and Crazy Horse split, seemingly for good.

Track Listing:

Mideast Vacation • Long Walk Home • Around The World • Inca Queen • Too Lonely • Prisoners Of Rock'n'Roll • Cryin' Eyes • When Your Lonely Heart Breaks • We Never Danced

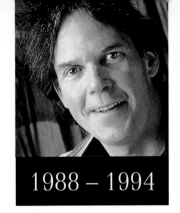

1988 – 1994

Second Harvest

en Men Workin' ', the opening shot on the Blue Notes' April 1988 debut, 'This Note's For You', showed a band with a purpose and their leader as a man with a mission:

> *We are men at work*
> *We got a job to do*
> *We got to keep you rockin'*
> *To keep your soul from the blue.*

The old gleam was back in Neil's eye, there was an extra spring in his heel. The black fedora and the shades suggested that, this time around, rock's most wayward son had re-invented himself as Blues Brother Jake Elwood. A cursory listen to his latest waxing – a set of bruising, big-band R&B tunes – would certainly confirm such a view.

'This Note's For You' was infused with the spirit of John Lee Hooker, BB King and Muddy Waters, though Neil was clearly a little too good-humoured to play the blues with that necessary authentic dash of inner torture, and the band sounded happiest on numbers like 'Sunny Inside' that recalled the classic Stax/Atlantic sound. The roundel on the bottom of the back sleeve – 'the dawn of power swing' – gave the game away.

The Blue Notes hit a high-energy groove from the off, the five-man horn section picking up on the swing riffs, using them to punctuate the guitar solos or to beef up the vocals. Young was in surprisingly good shape vocally, and his guitar playing equally hit the right spot, showing just how much he'd absorbed the phrasing of the great bluesmasters like Buddy Guy. On one cut, 'Hey Hey', he even broke with tradition and played a little slide guitar!

The tunes here, for the most part, addressed the usual obsessions of the blues form – women, infidelity, cars and work – but here and there Young flexed his formidable talent as a biting lyricist. 'Life In The City' was an essay on urban decay with its attendant problems of crime, poverty and homelessness, but even here the singer could offer no solution beyond his social concern.

The title cut, meanwhile, was to become the album's most notorious track, a broadside at corporate rock sponsorship that openly named the names of the worst offenders. But even

The Blue Notes' high-energy horns and guitars provided a great showcase for Young's lyrical talents, producing the likes of 'Life In The City' and the infamous 'This Note's For You'

Young admitted that this swipe at the likes of Budweiser and Miller was too idealistic, as he could never completely get around the situation at concerts where the promoters arranged the deal directly with the beer companies and he had no choice but to play them.

More controversial than the tune was the promotional video made by English director Julien Temple – best-known for chronicling the life and death of the Sex Pistols in *The Great Rock'n' Roll Swindle* and the film musical that really bombed, *Absolute Beginners*. The film, with its overt anti-sponsorship propaganda, had various send-ups of TV commercials that included designer Calvin Klein's male fragrance Obsession For Men (it's name now having changed to Concession!) and a climactic scene in

which a Whitney Houston clone tried to extinguish the burning hair of a Michael Jackson lookalike with Pepsi-Cola.

The video so incensed MTV (Neil had jabbed his finger at them elsewhere on the new album) that they immediately banned it on the grounds of its open 'product placement', but it was so well received that a year later the same corporation nominated it Best Video Of The Year at their music awards ceremony!

The song was a great live favourite, too, striking an immediate chord with cheering audiences who could identify with its sentiments. The Blue Notes were very much a live club band.

In their short time together, they toured extensively and a number of shows were recorded for a projected double LP, 'This Note's For You Too', which was later scrapped, as was a studio follow-up. A brand new composition, 'I'm Goin' ', later surfaced as the B-side of the US single of 'Ten Men Workin' ' as did a live version of 'This Note's For You' on a second single culled from the album – it offered those unfortunate to have missed out on Blue Notes concerts a rare glimpse of what was

one of Neil Young's hardest-working bands in their best environment.

Live performances during this period usually consisted of two basic one-hour selections that paid absolutely no lip-service to his past glories, but just concentrated on tracks from the album and on new songs such as 'Ordinary People' (which was an epic 15 minutes in length) and 'Sixty To Zero'. Even more remarkable were three tunes – 'Ain't It The Truth', 'Hello Lonely Woman' and 'Find Another Shoulder' – that had been written back in his school days at Kelvin High. They'd been gathering dust until rediscovered by ex-Squires bass player Ken Koblun, who then sent Young the old lyric sheets.

When duties with the Blue Notes permitted, recording continued at Young's ranch on the long-anticipated CSN&Y album. Crosby had finally cleaned up drug-wise, and this had been the main proviso of Young's agreement to work with them again. He'd publicly stated this in 1984 and proved a man of his word, but talking about the reunion some time later he made it sound very much an obligation:

'We made a record . . . but I've gone so far, I've gone all over the place and they're still doing what they've always done. Coming back together wasn't as easy as I thought it might be.' In view of such feelings and all the abortive sessions in the Seventies that had failed to produce a follow-up studio album to 'Déjà Vu', it was quite a feat then that they completed one in 1988. Rumours persisted, too, that Stephen Stills was now the one with the serious drug problems – he was so far gone that he was apparently under the delusion that he'd spent the Sixties serving in Vietnam!

Reunion

Once laughingly referred to by Neil as 'Geriatrics' Revenge', the reunion platter was issued on 21 November. 'American Dream' boasted 14 tracks, four of which (including the title song) were Young originals and a further two, 'Drivin' Thunder' and 'Night Song', were penned with Stills. The album was essentially insipid Adult Oriented Rock, lots of pretty harmony vocals but signally devoid of inspiration. Considering the radical changes in the world order and all the bloody little wars raging across the planet in the late Eighties, tunes like 'Soldiers Of Peace' sounded embarrassingly out of place – doubly so when one considered Crosby and Stills' fascination with guns! 'Drivin' Thunder' rocked well enough with some blistering slide work from Stills, while 'Old Black' (Neil's trusty Gibson) put some meat on the bones of the title track and blew up a storm with Stills again on 'Night Song'.

It was almost too predictable just to say that Neil Young's contributions shone out like the proverbial beacon. 'Feel Your Love' was Neil at his 'Harvest' best with just a simple acoustic guitar accompaniment and a beautiful lingering melody, the perfect panacea to the album's many overblown, synthetic moments. And 'This Old House' – emphatically not a retread of

Opposite: Neil Young's brief but dynamic alliance with the horn-led, rhythm and blues outfit the Blue Notes always worked best as a live attraction.

Above: Taking time out for a non-sponsored beverage

161

the Rosemary Clooney/Shakin' Stevens hit, but a peculiar rejoinder to Nash's 'Our House' – also beat the competition. On one level, with its tale of a family home being repossessed by the bank, it could have fitted in well with the maudlin 'Old Ways' collection, but its uncanny echo of the Nash tune gave it an unexpected barb. The harmonies sparkled, there was an effective use of organ behind the chorus and Neil's Hank Marvin-style guitar solo was a delight.

Restless

To celebrate the album's release, CSN&Y appeared at the Palace Theater in Hollywood on Young's birthday, and a month later at the Oakland Coliseum as part of a second benefit gig for the Bridge School – an all-acoustic affair that also starred Dylan, Tracy Chapman, Nils Lofgren, Tom Petty and Billy Idol! 1988 was a bumper year for awards – in September Young and the Blue Notes had won a 'Bammie' for Best Blues/Ethnic Band and in November he'd picked up the Silver Clef, awarded by the Nordoff-Robbins Music Therapy Organisation. In the January, too, he'd inducted Woody Guthrie, posthumously, into the Rock'n'Roll Hall Of Fame.

But awards weren't the only things Neil was collecting – fading Philadelphia soul star Harold Melvin successfully served a court injunction to prevent Young from using the Blue Notes name. The band, now Ten Men Working, were soon living up to their name and back on the road on a mini-tour of California. It was to be their last outing together as that line-up, and the chances of them ever reuniting with their boss again took a further blow when sax player Steve Lawrence sadly died of pneumonia in 1990.

Neil's spirit of artistic restlessness continued to rage. As Christmas approached, it could be denied no longer and he checked into New York's Hit Factory studios for an explosive burst of creativity which resulted in a whole album of new material, tentatively called 'Times Square' but then changed to

1988 saw the release of the long-awaited CSN&Y reunion album 'American Dream', and live performances by the group to celebrate Neil's birthday and at benefit gigs

'Eldorado'. Word got out that this latest extravaganza was a screaming holocaust of no-holds-barred, uncompromising, loud and devastating guitar rock, . . . but, true to form, it was to be consigned to the vaults.

Meanwhile he threw himself into more mini-tours, the band (now minus the horn section) known as the Restless (as in Neil Young and the Restless). During this period, he also found time to indulge his cinematic interest, following appearances in *68*, *Made In Heaven* and *Backtrack* with a cameo role as a gangster in Alan Rudolph's film noir, *Love At Large* alongside stars Tom Berenger and Anne Archer, shot in Oregon in the spring of 1989.

back on top form once again. 'Holocaustal, post-apocalypse ruptures and manglings, great bloody swathes of feedback, random distortions, and gashes of sound, the reckless weather of psychotic abandon. . . "Eldorado" is probably the greatest guitar rock album ever.'

If this was the much-hoped-for return to former glories, it was baffling that it should receive such a limited release. In Perth, Young cryptically explained over the radio that he liked to release EPs from time to time to let his fans know what he's been up to between albums. Later in the UK, he was more forthcoming. In an interview with Radio One's Richard Skinner, he suggested:

'If somebody really wants to hear it, they can always make a copy of it. This is the digital age. Go ahead, make a copy. I don't care.'

He then went on to explain to the DJ why the record had been put out in such truncated form:

'I recorded a lot of stuff, eight or nine songs, at the Hit Factory in New York on Times Square. And I put together an album called "Times Square", and then I changed the name to "Eldorado". And then I mastered it and then just as it was being readied for release I changed my mind about it because I thought I really wanted to have an album that was really gonna make an effect. That wasn't just gonna be something I wanted to do. I decided that I'd done what I wanted to do long enough and just doing that wasn't enough . . .

'I thought "Eldorado" by itself was a really fine album . . . But, you know, if you don't have a record they can play on the radio, you might as well forget it. You might as well not put out a record. So I took the songs that really created the feeling on "Eldorado" and put them out as an EP, therefore eliminating any crap that I have to go through with all of the radio stations and promotions and record companies and doing all these things to try and get it heard. I eliminated that by not even entering into the arena . . .

In April Neil and Co were Down Under playing shows across New Zealand and Australia and six dates in Japan under the guise of the Lost Dogs. Young had apparently lost his dog a few weeks beforehand and decided to bemoan this by renaming the band. The blues-based repertoire had been ditched – this tour saw a return to a full range of songs and many old favourites were sprinkled in among the obligatory newies.

Many of these were from the shelved 'Times Square' set. To promote the tour of the Antipodes, Reprise Records released a mini-album of some of the finest moments from these latest sessions as 'Eldorado'. . . and just to make it a little bit more special it was released on cassette and vinyl only in New Zealand and Australia, and on CD in Japan. The results had the critics reaching for their dictionaries for superlatives.

'Parts of it are like nothing you've ever heard,' ranted the *Melody Maker*'s Allan Jones, clearly relieved to find Young

'At least I didn't have to put myself through this exasperating experience of trying to get something I felt was really me on the radio only to find out over and over again that no one's gonna play it because it doesn't fit with some format. I mean I'm sick of that.'

Such fighting talk matched the fierce spirit of the five-track 'Eldorado' which, for fans of Neil's more 'abrasive' side, was manna from six-string heaven – 26 minutes of the most brutal, heavy guitar Young had to date committed to record. 'Cocaine Eyes' was a swirling sandstorm, a churning anti-drug rant building up on shard after shard of feedback – as the track opened, a voice presumably from the mixing desk shouted, 'that's loud' to which the maestro, ripping another deafening riff from 'Old Black', replied, 'Yeah! Sounds good though. Let's try one like that.'

More gut-wrenching guitar thuggery followed, on 'Don't Cry' ('a song about a girl and a boy breaking up') and 'Heavy Love'. Some respite might have been expected from Neil's version of the Drifters' 'On Broadway' hit – but, ornery critter that he was, he savaged the life out of it, the crushing guitar riffs and

relentless rhythm squeezing the marrow out of its bones. You could only breath a sigh of relief as Spanish guitars signalled the title track, full of Mexican images that evoked the poetic grandeur of Sam Peckinpah's finest films – a shame the two never got to work together.

'Eldorado''s guitar-strangling mania rather put another very worthy effort in the shade. This was 'The Bridge', a Neil Young tribute LP issued by US label, No 6 Records, in July, featuring many of the Eighties' feistiest young rockers including the Pixies, Sonic Youth, Dinosaur Jr and the not-so-young Nick Cave wrapping his tonsils around 'Helpless'. Through the mid-Eighties, such dedicatory albums were all the rage, with the Manchester-based Imaginary label leading the field when it honoured the likes of Syd Barrett, the Kinks, Captain Beefheart and the Rolling Stones.

Building Bridges

These had clearly influenced the album's executive producer, Terry Tolkin, who felt he could do a better job on Young. 'I felt all of them were brilliant ideas,' he told *Broken Arrow*, 'but that they were poorly executed. . . I decided to commission all new interpretations of Neil's tunes because I wanted the various artists I approached to feel extra special about their contribution. To be able to record their track with a sense of purpose.'

The idea had first taken root when he'd seen the Church jamming with Tom Verlaine (the leader of the influential Television, a band also inspired by Young) on 'Cortez The Killer' – he subsequently tried but failed (apparently due to lack of interest from the Church's management) to feature this inspired union on the album.

Nonetheless 'The Bridge' sold well with profits being channelled into a school of the same name Young had set up for severely handicapped children. Young's first reactions to the tribute were predictably ambiguous, as he told *Q* magazine:

'I love those people and it's nice that they did that but I'm not ready for that. They don't mean to close the book, but to me it's still threatening.' He'd mellowed towards it a year or so later, as he confided to *Vox*'s Nick Kent:

'I love that record now. Before, I sort of saw it as all these groups saying, "OK, Uncle Neil, time for that rocking chair." But I love all those guys on the record – the Pixies, Sonic Youth and that Nick Cave guy in particular. When I heard it, it really touched me.'

'The Bridge' was a timely reassessment of the career of one of rock'n'roll's few surviving genii – Neil was moving back into the public's consciousness, and his recent artistic returns to form were about to receive a further boost before the year was out. But meanwhile he continued to tour with the vigour of a 17-year-old.

This time it was a solo acoustic trek, though before long long-time pals Ben Keith and Poncho were joining him on stage for some of the set. The road led him from California across to the East Coast and three weeks later he wrapped up the tour in Denver. It was in this final, trio format that European audiences were to enjoy him in December, on a nine-day whistle-stop tour through Italy, Germany, Holland, France and climaxing with well-received shows at London's Hammersmith Odeon. According to Sampedro these dates were a last-minute decision, Young springing news of the tour on the hapless guitarist as they flew home from New York on 15 November.

Young was happy to raid his awesome back catalogue for these shows, with the occasional unheard gem thrown in. These included the soon-to-become-legendary 'F*!#in' Up', a distorted acoustic romp which rather threw audiences waiting for the more familiar territory of 'After The Goldrush' and 'Heart Of Gold'. And he was clearly inspired by the momentous events that were reshaping the world at the end of the decade, ending his set with a message.

Opposite: Acknowledging his loyal fans

Above: The combination of harmonica and Young's similarly keening voice has always been one of the most affecting sounds in rock

'I'd like to finish off here with a song for the little Chinese boy. A song that should be forgotten. It's for this little Chinese boy with a flower in his hand; you saw him on TV, standing in front of the tanks. It made quite an impression, a paper maché statue up there. It was pretty big, the last I saw of that it was falling over. But apparently the Chinese leaders are into television and they got the tapes and they recognised that little Chinese boy, so this song's for him'...and, with the chilling images of Tiananmen Square flashing through his mind, he tore into 'Ohio', nearly 20 years old but terrifyingly relevant.

Freedom

The core of these shows comprised many of the songs that had just been released as 'Freedom', a record which would have *Melody Maker* reporter Everett True proclaiming 'candidate for Album Of The Year'. (It was in *Rolling Stone* magazine!) 'Freedom' was 'slightly pasteurised', as Neil put it, elaborating on his comments to Richard Skinner about the concept of 'Eldorado', which had been streamlined for maximum media impact. He'd pieced the resultant hour-long work together from a mind-boggling array of different sessions, three cuts from the 'Eldorado' EP, one from the 'Times Square' project, two from a possible second studio set by the Blue Notes, a couple of duets with Linda Ronstadt (back with Neil for the first time since 'American Stars'n'Bars') and some recordings where he was backed up by the Lost Dogs.

In the tradition of 'Tonight's The Night' and 'Rust Never Sleeps', 'Freedom' began and ended with the same tune, 'Rockin' In The Free World', a live acoustic opening shot being followed by a full-blown snarling electric closer with the Dogs

Left: Young performing with the Blue Notes in New York City in 1988

Opposite: A live acoustic version of 'Rockin' In The Free World', issued in 1989

yapping up a storm. 'Rockin'' took an ironic second look at the American Dream he'd been so quick to promote during the Reagan era. In his confusion, Young confronted the age-old chestnut, what price freedom? What was the point of America's overseas wars defending the notion of 'democracy', when she'd got a real mess in her own backyard – drug abuse, religious bigotry, violent crime, homelessness and poverty? The song's bitter-sweet, double-edged commentary wasn't lost on those who seized upon it as something of an anthem in the wake of the Berlin Wall being torn down and the subsequent collapse of the Iron Curtain.

These themes were explored further on other tracks, notably on 'Crime In The City (Sixty To Zero Part 1)' which the Blue Notes had been performing with its full 11 verses (here reduced to four), and on the fuzz-drenched, stark rendition of 'On Broadway' where Young brought out the song's true message of squalor – especially the howled 'Give me that crack, give me some of that crack' in the song's dying throes. It prompted some fans to wonder whether he'd embellished the Drifters' original with an extra verse – he hadn't. As he explained in *Broken Arrow* magazine, 'the lyrics are exactly the same as the original'. These themes were reflected in a video promo of the 'Rockin'' track – again directed by Julien Temple – which depicted Young dressed as a bum in downtown Los Angeles, drifting between skid row and the nearby yuppie financial district.

One of 'Freedom''s most curious selections was 'Don't Cry', a track which had also been part of the heavy-duty 'Eldorado' EP. Discussing his admiration for the late Roy Orbison, he told journalist Nick Kent:

'I've always put a piece of Roy Orbison on every album I've ever made. His influence is on so many of my songs . . . I even had his photograph on the sleeve of "Tonight's The Night". Just recognising his presence. There's a big Orbison tribute song on "Eldorado" called "Don't Cry". That's totally me under the Roy Orbison . . . spell. When I wrote it and then recorded it, I was thinking, "Roy Orbison meets trash metal." (laughs) Seriously!'

Impressive though it was, this latest set was somewhat disappointing for hardened Young fans. It didn't, for instance, contain 'Box Car', performed live in recent times and part of the Hit Factory beanfeast – and, worse still, 'Ordinary People', the epic, poetry-crammed tour de force, which he now contrarily thought had 'dated too quickly...(as) too topical'. But perhaps 'Freedom''s main point of significance was that it saw its maker reconnecting his soul with a world he had shut the door on since 1979, and finally breaking free from his various domestic trials.

'It did maybe close me down a little in my feelings,' he admitted to Adam Sweeting in the *Guardian*, 'because it hurt so much to have that happen that I had to deny that it happened, to some extent. You can't just stop feeling one thing. When you stop feeling, you stop feeling everything. I think that happened to me for a while. And so my music didn't reflect my innermost feelings for a while.'

As he entered a fourth decade of musical endeavour, his breakneck pace showed no sign of slowing. He was still preparing the ever more ambitious retrospective, 'Decade II', which was now drawing on a staggering 20 unreleased albums, and a video to go with it. He also helped out Warren Zevon again on his 'Transverse City' album, adding harmony

Young in full flight at London's Hammersmith Odeon in 1989.
He has always preferred to play smaller venues rather than the
aircraft hangar-sized arenas

vocals to 'Splendid Isolation' and some rumbling lead guitar on 'Gridlock'. Tracy Chapman shared the same management as Young, a connection that saw him contribute acoustic guitar and piano to 'All That You Have Is Your Soul' from her 'Crossroads' album.

On 10 November 1989, two days before the singer's 44th birthday, Much Music (Canada's answer to MTV) broadcast a one-hour retrospective special which comprised video clips, concert footage, interviews (including a recent one with Young on his ranch) and location shots of his Winnipeg roots. It showed the old rogue in humorous, loquacious vein, candid about the fraught Geffen years, but still typically defiant in the face of corporate rock:

'Selling a lot of records is not satisfying,' he spat. 'Playing to the people is satisfying. That's what I'm here for. I live for playing live.'

Prophetic words! There were no end of good causes he wanted to support. When the California earthquakes had wreaked disaster on the West Coast, he'd offered his services to one of three relief benefits organised by promoter Bill Graham. Young played a solo set at San Francisco's Cow Palace in November 1989 on a bill which included CS&N, America and the Steve Miller Band, the night ending with an extended blues jam with Miller and various members of his band being joined by Carlos Santana, Taj Mahal, the Chambers Brothers and Neil on piano.

An appearance with CS&N in March at a benefit gig in LA for their old drummer, Dallas Taylor, now critically ill, was quickly followed up by one at Farm Aid 4 at the Hoosier Dome, Indianapolis, on 7 April: CS&N sang 'Suite: Judy Blue Eyes' before being joined by Neil for 'This Old House'. Young also performed a couple of solo songs – 'Rockin' In The Free World' and a new one, 'Freedom Now'. Nine days later he flew across the Atlantic for the International Tribute to Nelson Mandela at London's Wembley Stadium, where once more his anthemic 'Rockin' In The Free World' stole the show.

In this head-spinning whirl of live appearances, spring 1990 brought with it another creative rush. The material, Young reasoned, could only be played by one band – Crazy Horse.

Ragged Glories

It had come to light that one of the reasons for their 1987 divorce from Young had apparently been Billy Talbot's prodigious drinking – Ralph Molina had even tried out for the Blue Notes rhythm section with another old Horse refugee, George Whitsell, until Young had plumped for Messrs Rosas and Cromwell. And 'Poncho' had never left Neil's fold.

After a period of inactivity, Crazy Horse had begun pulling themselves back into shape. They'd been joined by Sonny Mone, a singer/guitarist who'd made the career move from playing the dives of New England to those of Los Angeles, where he was befriended by Talbot. Adding the icing to the cake was lead guitarist Matt Piucci, who was picking himself up out of the ashes of the Rain Parade. The Parade were one of the finest bands to come out of the West Coast since the Sixties, shaping a gorgeous, folk-flavoured psychedelic rock from the anvil of LA's punk scene. Matt's mercurial playing was legion among aficionados of the Parade for its fiery beauty that owed much of its inspiration to two prime sources, Tom Verlaine . . . and Neil Young!

He was a perfect candidate for the job, and the quartet were soon out playing the bars. They also started to record, predominantly Mone numbers, and, through Piucci, were

signed up to Pat Thomas's small Heyday label; San Francisco-based, it specialised in folk rock, including solo records from various ex-members of Green On Red and the Rain Parade. The self-deprecatingly titled 'Left For Dead' emerged in early 1989 but Capitol Records, smelling big bucks, took the record over and re-released it some months later on their Sisapa subsidiary label.

Surprisingly, then, and after the solid excellence of 'Crazy Moon' (11 years before!), this new waxing was nothing to write home about. Yes, many of the familiar Horse trademarks were there – the great chugging rhythm sound and Piucci's incisive lead, which more than compensated for the absence of both Whitten and Young. But where were the songs? The seven Mone-written tunes were all bar-room rockers that followed the same basic pattern. His 'Mountain Man' was only notable for having been originally dedicated to Young. Where were songs like Talbot's latest ditties, 'Show A Little Faith', 'World Of Love' and 'I Could Never Lose Your Love'?

The best they could come up with was a Talbot-Piucci tune, 'You And I' which reflected Matt's fine ear for melody. Why the guitarist didn't feature more in the credits, considering his contributions to the Rain Parade, was all the more mystifying. A subsequent single, 'Child Of War' – a driving, neo-metal rocker with heartfelt lyrics – partially made up for the album's more turgid moments, and was promoted by a video of the band playing interspersed with film clips of man's inhumanity to man.

All this Crazy Horse activity meant that one of the greatest engine rooms in the history of rock'n'roll was turning over and ready to give Young's new tunes the lift they needed when Messrs Talbot and Molina arrived at the ranch in April 1990.

Overleaf: Stealing the show with the anthemic 'Rockin' In The Free World' during the International Tribute to Nelson Mandela at London's Wembley Stadium in spring 1990

Neil Young at centre stage during the spectacular finale of the 1990 Farm Aid benefit, with veteran country outlaw Willie Nelson (second right)

'Billy Talbot is a massive bass player who only plays two or three notes,' Young would later comment. 'People are still trying to figure out whether it's because he only knows two or three notes or whether those are the only notes he wants to play. But when he hits a note, that note speaks for itself. It's a big motherf***ing note. Even the soft one is big. Without Crazy Horse playing so big, I sound just normal. But they are big so I can float around and sound huge'. Producer David Briggs who'd been responsible for all of Neil and Crazy Horse's greatest moments together – 'Everybody Knows This Is Nowhere', 'Zuma' and 'Rust Never Sleeps' – was back at the control desk, and it was time to get down to some serious rock'n'roll. Neil meant business – and when the results of this latest liaison were released in September 1990, they found the crusty old buzzard in sheer f***-you bloody-minded mood.

It was as if Young had taken umbrage at rock's latest wave of youthful pretenders pouring out of Seattle (Mudhoney, Nirvana and their ilk) and had decided to give 'em a taste of their own guitar grunge medicine. The urge to show them who was still boss must have been strong as images of these young men with long, lank locks, ripped jeans, check work-shirts and electric guitars (the prototype Young image for 20 years!) flickered through his mind. 'Ragged Glory' was a fabulously charged affair – after the sad attempts to get it right with the Horse on Eighties albums, the excitement flowed from its opening bars.

Its gun-slingin' guitar work-outs might have been just what the doctor ordered for half-starved fans, but this was no mere sop on Young's behalf. Many of the numbers here faded with long feedback guitar passages, as if thumbing his nose once again at the system of radio promotion: indeed, two of the numbers clocked in at an epic 10 minutes apiece. However, the shit-kicking, gut-bender 'Don't Spook The Horse' from the same sessions was conspicuous by its absence, turning up only on the US 'Mansion On The Hill' CD single.

This truculence was topped by the anthemic 'F*!#in' Up', the formerly acoustic outing given an almost Frankenstein-like new lease of life from Crazy Horse's lightning-bolt power. It was one of the album's catchiest cuts and, with its call-and-response chorus, was to become an integral part of Young's repertoire – but stood zero chance of airplay! Below its humorous surface lurked a set of nightmarish lyrics, snapshot lines as dark and mysterious as any Young had written.

For all its guitar-crushing pyrotechnics, most notably the speed-metal burn-out on the old Don & Dewey garage classic 'Farmer John', 'Ragged Glory' delivered on the word front, too. 'Mansion On The Hill' looked as if Neil was reconsidering his hard-line stance on the Sixties which had taken such a beating on odes like 'Hippie Dream' and 'Ambulance Blues'. This time around, he seemed to feel the need to return to the old sentiments espoused by the peace'n'love generation. Maybe in the turbulent present, they still offered hope after all.

> There's a mansion on the hill
> Psychedelic music fills the air
> Peace and love live there still
> In that mansion on the hill.

'Mother Earth (Natural Anthem)', also known as 'Freedom Man', was another track that caught this sudden return to the old ideals and values – another of those rare green moments (as on 'After The Goldrush') where Neil, amid a cacophonous wail of feedback, pleaded for an end to the corporate destruc-tion of the planet. However, the real clue to Young's state of mind was to be found in 'Days That Used To Be', which ached with a crippling disillusionment with the present.

On 'Ragged Glory', Young was vanquishing the latest troupe of monkeys on his back with some good old physical exercise – the virile sonic guitar duels, the wallowing in nature's needs (it was no surprise to note that sex was preying deeply on his mind on this album – 'Over And Over', 'Farmer John', 'Don't Spook The Horse' etc). And if you looked close enough at the credits on the inner sleeve, you saw that Mike Moran, Neil's PT teacher, even got a credit!!

Smell the Horse

The album was followed by some promotional videos for 'F*!#in' Up', 'Mansion On The Hill', 'Farmer John' and 'Over And Over', which caught the quartet in sleazy mood – one of the films saw Young shoving his guitar down a toilet bowl, while the two directed by Rusty Cunclieff were equally bizarre. For 'Farmer John', the band masqueraded as Denver cabbies, while 'Mansion', a pastiche of the award-winning *Driving Miss Daisy*, saw Young as a mechanic, a priest and finally rising from the dead!

It was just as well that the singer was keeping in good shape – another benefit show for the Bridge School required his services on 26 October where he joined Elvis Costello for his own set encore of 'Alison' (Elvis returning the compliment by later appearing on 'Down By the River'). The Steve Miller Band, Jackson Browne, Edie Brickell, compere Cheech Marin and of course Young and Crazy Horse rounded off the bill. And a month later Young and the Horse were stalking the boards in a more familiar setting, the Catalyst in Santa Cruz, no doubt as a warm-up for their soon-to-come winter tour.

During an evening that saw these guitar-totin' desperadoes deliver three loud'n'fast sets, there were one or two surprises, the quartet disinterring some long-forgotten 'Zuma' favourites

– 'Don't Cry No Tears', 'Cortez' and 'Danger Bird'. The Santa Cruz anthem, 'Homegrown', had the crowd goin' ape and Young even liberated a couple of 'Re.Ac.Tor' s still-borns, 'Surfer Joe' and 'T-bone'.

The ensuing cross-country trek, now dubbed the 'Smell the Horse' tour was scheduled to start at the Target Centre, Minneapolis, on 22 January 1991. And Young had chosen the support acts, Sonic Youth and Social Distortion, with typical native wit and wisdom.

'I didn't want any acts that people were going to say, "Oh, I can take 'em or leave 'em",' he told *Melody Maker*. 'I wanted to get somebody that people were going to love or hate. And I think we did a good job there. Sonic Youth are way out there on the cutting edge . . . extremely similar to what we've been doing for a long time.

While the band rehearsed at Prince's Paisley Park studios, events in the 'real' world unexpectedly intervened. As the United Nations' 15 January deadline for Iraqi President Saddam Hussein to pull his troops out of Kuwait expired, the American-led Allies unleashed their counter-attack. The first rounds of Operation Desert Storm were devastating air strikes on Kuwait City and Baghdad, and media coverage, especially that of TV channel CNN, was almost as intense as the blanket-bombing in the Middle East. Whatever one's personal feeling about the Gulf War might have been, there was no denying the powerful emotions stirred by this news coverage overkill.

Recognising the complexity of the situation – the anger with which the world viewed Iraq's dictator for his premeditated invasion of a small neighbouring state, the concern for the men sent to the frontline to fight, the wholesale slaughter of that dictator's people who had never even had a chance to

elect him in the first place, and the frightening, incalculable environmental impact the war would have – the singer felt he had to do something. The set list was overhauled, songs like 'Cortez' and 'Powderfinger' (catalogues of pillage, invasion, the loss of young life) taking the place of tunes from the 'Ragged Glory' album. He even roped in Dylan's hoary old protest song, 'Blowin' In The Wind', while on stage the old CND peace sign fluttered on a black backdrop behind Ralph Molina's drum rise.

Last but not least, tied to the giant mike stand left over from the 'Rust' tour was a solitary yellow ribbon.

Young could offer no solution to the war, although Jimi Hendrix's trusty Woodstock re-construction of the American national anthem continued to open the shows and seemed to suggest that the US had still not learned anything from its Vietnam debacle. (Ironically, the 'Star-Spangled Banner' was misinterpreted by some audiences who took it at face value as a mark of simple patriotism.) Later in the year, when the war was over, Young unburdened himself to *Melody Maker*.

'It blew my head off during that tour. When we were playing that stuff, it was intense. It was real. I could see people dying in my mind. I could see bombs falling, buildings collapsing on families. We were watching CNN all the time, watching this shit happen, and then going out to play, singing these songs about conflict. I feel there was nothing else I could do . . .

'As soon as the war started, I changed the set list. A few "Ragged Glory" songs were replaced with older songs that I knew people could relate to. I knew people would be unified. Whatever could bring people together was far more important than me playing a new song. We couldn't go out there and just be entertainment. It would have been in bad taste.'

This series of concerts were carried away on tidal waves of psychic energy which welded together all the disparate forces at work in the venues. Up on stage art was imitating life, the flame-thrower guitars inextinguishable as a ruptured oil-well, the Crazy Horse rhythms as relentless as the tank treads crawling across the desert, howling feedback raining down like a cluster of Cruise missiles, Molina's percussive bomb-blasts exploding with the impact of a downed jet. It mirrored the audience's hopes and fears as world peace hung in the balance halfway across the globe.

Reviewing the Madison Square Garden show for *Melody Maker*, Simon Reynolds eloquently described Young's music as

Opposite: The choice of noise merchants Sonic Youth to support Crazy Horse on their 'Smell The Horse' tour of 1991 proved an inspired one

Above: The Horse take a well-deserved bow on stage

lying 'in the slipstream of the two great American traumatic disillusionments: the closing of the frontier at the end of the 19th century and the closing of the psychological/existential frontier opened up in the late Sixties', but he must have missed the smaller logo tucked away on stage between the amps: Rebecca Holland's painting of one of the West's most potent figures, the man whose name Young had used for his own backing band, Chief Crazy Horse.

This was the real clue to the 'mythical resonance' invested in Young and band. Like the great Lakota Sioux chief, they were 'battered heroic survivors of a grander age' who, instead of fighting the encroachments of the soldiers and the settlers to retain the freedom of their nomadic lifestyle, were fighting to keep music free of the corporate rock machine and all its attendant evils that threatened to destroy it – sponsorship, merchandising, advertising, conformity. The blood-curdling Sioux war whoop that prefaced the rendition of 'F*!#in' Up' reinforced this!

The 'Smell The Horse' tour wound up after a gruelling 54 performances, each of two hours plus – and, despite his emphasis on physical fitness, it understandably left Young exhausted. Resting up, he turned his attention to producing both an aural and a visual documentary of these nerve-shredding shows that, he told *Melody Maker*, 'left me stunned... There wasn't one night that was less than intense. It was intense from beginning to end and it never let up.'

A double album, 'Weld', based on the 'Horse' tour and, the teeth-clenched, funereal version of 'Blowin' In The Wind' aside, offering no new numbers, was released in November. But unlike 'Live Rust', his last, less than riveting live double, 'Weld' was an emotional volcano that pinned down the listener from the opening mortar attack of 'Hey Hey My My' and just kept on coming.

With no sign of a ceasefire for a further two hours, it was like standing in the centre of the war zone as Young and Sampedro's guitars strafed track after track with aural shrapnel from a deranged fuzz-box holocaust. The overriding feeling of approaching Armageddon created by the Gulf conflict had breathed new life into old warhorses that had been kicking around the Young 'rust bucket' for longer than even he cared to remember.

Highlights are hard to extract from a set that has to be viewed as a cohesive whole – but it's impossible to ignore 'Like A Hurricane' which weighed in at an epic 15 minutes and took off just as it should have back on 'Stars'n'Bars'. Naturally, more patient fans waited for the accompanying video, directed by Young himself (using his cinematic alias of Bernard Shakey), who intercut concert footage with frightening images from the war. There was nothing new about this – British director Tony Palmer had originated this iconoclastic style back in 1969 when he married psychedelic rock'n'roll with footage from the Vietnam War and the Paris riots. But Neil and Crazy Horse performing at such an intense level, suddenly intercut with the sight of Baghdad burning, still made for a powerful experience.

Deconstruction

'Weld' was released as a limited edition with another CD, 'Arc', a 35-minute orgy of orchestrated guitar feedback somewhere between Lou Reed's 'Metal Machine Music' and British band Spacemen 3's long, scorching, guitar-drone mantras. As Young revealed to *Melody Maker*, the idea for 'Arc' came from Sonic Youth's Thurston Moore. During the 'Horse' tour, Young had given him a copy of the still-to-be-released *Muddy Track* video, the film Young had shot on the bitter European tour back in 1987 when he and Crazy Horse had almost split up for good. Its soundtrack was made up of abrasive guitar intros and squealing feedback outros:

'There were shots of the road, moving back and forth, and then this distorted sound. That was the first time I isolated it and took all those things out. I really enjoyed that and I think that, in some way, it is the essence of what the song is about, those things we do at the beginning and the end. Thurston came back and said, "Wow, you guys ought to make a whole record of this stuff."'

And that was the origin of the 'Arc' concept. Young then went on to explain that there was a systematic logic to the way in which he'd assembled it from the 'Smell The Horse' concerts:

'There is an order to it. I took 57 pieces that we called "sparks". We took them out, numbered them and disassociated them from the concerts that they came from. Of those 57 pieces, I chose 37. I had them all on a database and I had all the keys and the lyrics that were in each piece all written down, and the location of the piece so I could tell what hall it was from, so that I could move from one hall to another so the sound wouldn't change radically.'

The result is a surprisingly fluid, circular concerto of disembodied guitar electronics, parts of which – like the sudden refrain of 'Like A Hurricane' and the disconcerting jazz lick from 'Tonight's The Night' – create ghostly, ambient moods. For Young it was a real innovation, once again revealing him determined never to sit still and proof again that even the younger breed of six-string deconstructionalists could learn a thing or two from the master! His intention for 'Arc' was for it to be played in clubs between records:

'Just put "Arc" on, play a record, fade "Arc" up for a while, fade it down, play another record. Have it on between bands. It's refreshing. It clears the palate. Because of the fact that there's no beat. It's not an insult to your sensitivity in what kind of a groove you dig. There is no groove. F*** that!'

Performing at Meadowlands in the USA, February 1991 – one of a series of intense concerts whose set reflected Young's concern with the newly-begun Gulf War

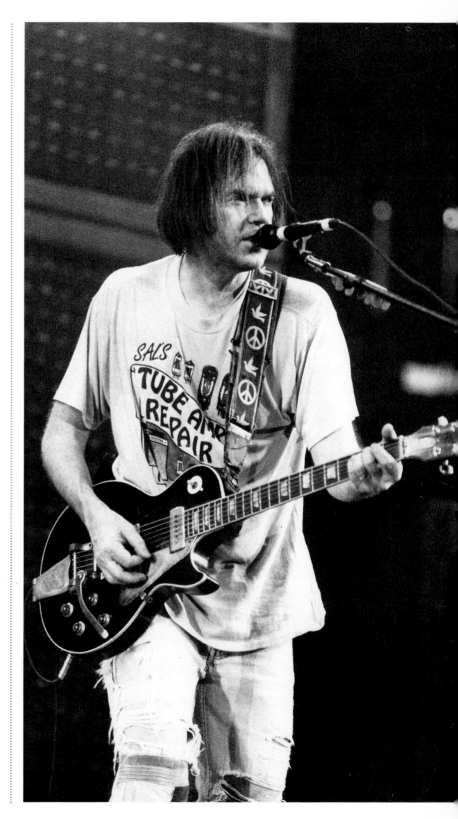

The release of 'Arc' / 'Weld' saw another cycle in the Young-Crazy Horse relationship close. As 1992 dawned, Young was once again contemplating an acoustic retreat, and Crazy Horse were relegated to the back-burner.

'I love Crazy Horse,' he insisted. 'I hope I'm playing with them as long as we're still alive. But I won't play with them on every record. And I can't play with them on every tour. There are too many sides to my music that I have to keep happening. And, if it wasn't for the other things I did, Crazy Horse wouldn't be so good.'

Second Harvest

In late November 1991, he began work on a new album – and from the outset, this was intended as a belated sequel to his most popular record, 'Harvest'. It was a course of action he'd been advised to follow for 20 years but, ever the renegade, Young displayed a testy contrariness when *Melody Maker* caught up with him at the time of release a year later and asked him whether this new album – titled 'Harvest Moon', and with the Stray Gators once more in attendance – was indeed the formal follow-up to his 1972 best-seller:

'They can call it whatever the hell they like,' he snorted. 'I just make these records. It's not my job to describe them as well . . . I never really said, "Yeah, let's do a sequel." It wasn't that worked out. In the beginning it was just another group of songs with just another buncha musicians. You know, I had these songs and then when I decided which musicians to use on them, I realised it was the same people I'd worked with on "Harvest". And whatever happened, happened.'

For all Young's evasiveness, 'Harvest Moon' did conjure up the gentle, introspective mood of its predecessor. It caught him in romantic, even nostalgic frame of mind, the troubadour with the broken heart. The dominant theme seemed to be about loss and the need to carry on, a theme he confirmed when talking to *Melody Maker*'s Allan Jones.

'I think the album's saying that it's okay that some things don't last forever. It doesn't mean you have to stop living or loving or experiencing things. You can still be as bright and into things as you were when you were young. It doesn't matter if you're 20, 30 or 40, whatever. The idea is to keep living. Don't snuff yourself out.'

'One Of These Days' saw Young looking back at all the friends and colleagues he'd left behind on the human highway, wishing that he could get back in touch with them, but realising that the future beckons and that he probably won't. 'From Hank To Hendrix' was also informed by the lure of the past and the need to go on. It looked back fondly on early musical influences, but with the line 'Here I am with this old guitar doing what I do' reaffirmed his commitment to life and music.

Not even the death of his pet dog, Elvis, could dim his spirit of continuance – instead he humorously paid tribute to the departed canine on 'Old King'. Meanwhile, 'You And Me', 'Such A Woman' and the title cut were musical love letters to his wife, celebrating the strengths of their long and close relationship with each other. All were sung with a heartfelt conviction.

The gentle folkiness of this latest album recalled the warm, sunny textures of 'Comes A Time', with its softly-strummed guitars, melancholic harmonica, mournful pedal steel and gorgeous harmony vocals. 'Harvest Moon' reunited him with singer Nicolette Larson whose work with Young in the late Seventies had given the inspired pairing of Dylan and Emmylou Harris (on the acclaimed 'Desire' album) more than a run for their money.

Larson was in angelic form, crooning especially sweetly in the duet of 'You And Me' and on the choruses of the 10-minute 'Natural Beauty', recorded live in Oregon. The album's closer, it reiterated many of the same concerns that had characterised 'After The Goldrush' – that no matter how much loss we suffer, be it broken relationships or destruction of the planet, life has to go on.

While the ambitious preparations for 'Harvest Moon' were taking place, Young took to the road, solo and acoustic, armed with a battery of guitars, harmonicas and pipe organ. He saw it as an ideal opportunity to try out the new songs. The very personal obsessions that would dominate the forthcoming album spilled over into his live act. And when an over-zealous fan interrupted his flow at the Beacon Theater in New York, Young – never an over-talkative performer on stage – took the opportunity to lecture his audience about the relationship between the past and the present. 'Y'know, every song was new once,' he observed. 'When I first came to New York, I played at the Bitter End and at Carnegie Hall and I was playing as many new songs then as I am now. The people who think they love me don't realise they're trying to stop me from going ahead.'

Neil Young on stage with the man himself at the 'Bobfest', Columbia's tribute to the music of Bob Dylan at Madison Square Garden in October 1992

It was a reminder, too, of his 'rust never sleeps' philosophy. Young was never one to let the grass grow underneath his musical feet. 1992 also had him supporting yet another Farm Aid benefit, collecting an honorary degree in music from the University of Ontario in Thunder Bay and in the autumn, appearing at what he christened the 'Bobfest'.

Dylan and Young stand as twin peaks in the roll call of North American rock – something the Canadian clearly recognised. 'We've come through a lot, people like Dylan, me, Lou Reed,' he said, believing all three have 'something out there that sweeps through us, that's completely out of our control'.

On 16 October 1992, the great and the good (and sundry hangers-on) of the American music business joined together in New York City in front of 18,000 rampant fans to pay tribute to three decades of Bob Dylan...and Neil Young's presence at the event in Madison Square Garden was not a surprise. After all, he'd been one of the star turns at the Band's Last Waltz some decade and a half earlier.

'It was great,' he said of the rather grandly titled 'Columbia Records Celebrates The Music Of Bob Dylan', 'met a lot of friends and it was a lotta fun'. But for most observers, the event's talking point had been the crowd's bizarre treatment of Sinead O'Connor, holder of controversial views on America and the Catholic faith, who left the stage in tears having endured what one magazine called 'perhaps the longest two minutes in showbiz history'.

With a line-up running from Booker T and the MGs through Stevie Wonder to Roger McGuinn and Lou Reed, the show included almost anyone who ever had a hit with a Dylan song and plenty that hadn't. Neil waited patiently in line, following O'Connor's furious rant through Bob Marley's 'War' (wrong Bob, Sinead!) with a smirk and a shout. 'This song's for you Bob – thanks for having Bobfest!' he yelped as the band behind him clattered into 'Just Like Tom Thumb's Blues' from 'Highway 61 Revisited'.

And, as one of the stars accorded another bite at the cherry, he encored with a version of 'All Along The Watchtower' that nodded to both Bob Dylan and Jimi Hendrix before quitting the Madison Square stage to make way for Chrissie Hynde and a change of pace. Irreverent but respectful to the last, Neil Young had managed to put his own personal stamp on the night's proceedings . . . with a smile.

His Les Paul guitar displays a customised tremelo arm, but the workshirt remains the same: Neil Young in the Nineties is one of rock's most familiar and trusted sights

Young elaborated a week or so later to *Melody Maker* on his affinity with Dylan: 'Bob was booed for playing electric, I was booed for coming on and singing with a vocoder and synth. I was booed in London, I was booed in Germany, Spain, France, Italy, everywhere.' But like Dylan and unlike O'Connor, he insisted 'they never made me run'.

Unplugged

A Dylan song had played a large part in the 1991 tour recorded for 'Weld': 'Blowin' In The Wind', played every night with an electric intensity even a post-Newport Zimmerman had rarely approached. *Melody Maker*'s New York correspondent, David Fricke, had described it as 'more firefight than storm warning, Dylan's measured acoustic query about peace and destiny jacked up with magnum electrical force and unmistakeable desperation as Young, Sampedro and Talbot raised their voices in tremulous pleading harmony'. It was, concluded Fricke, 'epic arena rock theatre'.

Young's choice was potent in view of the Gulf War raging at the time: 'The song itself asks the same questions everyone was asking then about how long it will be before people can be free. There was no other choice for me. That was the song.'

A year later, he returned to the stage resplendent in blue check workshirt, his black Les Paul dangling from a guitar strap sporting peace signs and doves, to take up position at Dylan's left shoulder for 'Knockin' On Heaven's Door'. It might not have been epic rock theatre this time, but judging by the width of the grin, it sure was fun!

The Bobfest was one more clear indication of Young's elevated place among the gods of rock's Mount Olympus. After all the plaudits for 'Harvest Moon', he must have been wondering where he was headed next. The short-term solution to this dilemma came from the unlikely source of MTV, a company often the target of his corporate rock sniping in the past. Young was asked to participate in their *Unplugged* series, which spotlighted major artists in a semi-acoustic setting. Eric Clapton, Nirvana, REM and 10,000 Maniacs were just some of the acts to feature in the first years of what was generally regarded as a prestigious show, while Clapton and Rod Stewart issued best-selling albums of their appearances. Filmed in Los Angeles, this TV special presented us with a comfortingly familiar image of the grizzled rock veteran.

A casually dressed and bearded Young sauntered on set, furrowing his brow as he sat down and prepared to grapple with an acoustic guitar every bit as worn as his leather jacket. The ever-present harmonica was soon brought into play for 'The Old Laughing Lady', a blast from the past from his first album which, unlike the song that followed hard on its heels, went unrecognised.

Deep harmonica howls scarred the surface of 'Mr Soul', the well-travelled Buffalo Springfield classic now exhumed in acoustic form following the heavy, computerised reworking it had received for 'Trans' a decade earlier and greeted, on this occasion, by fulsome applause.

By 'World On A String' Neil seemed wilfully to be avoiding eye contact with the camera . . . or was he transported back into the mid-Seventies void of 'Tonight's The Night'? The first truly stirring performance of this particular night came when he moved on to 'Rust Never Sleeps': 'Pocahontas' saw him strap on a 12-string, emphatically rasping forth the 'Brando, Pocahontas and me' refrain to rapturous and well-deserved applause.

Next up was 'Stringman', debuted in 1976 and originally recorded for the unreleased 'Chrome Dreams', which saw him turn to the piano for the first time. Its appearance on the album that followed this broadcast would be its first in legal form. Then a shift sideways, with a wry exclamation – his first major speech to the audience – of 'Scotty, I need more power', accompanied much clicking of switches on an ancient pedal-powered wind organ. USS Enterprise it wasn't . . .

Above: Postcard for the 'Unplugged' album, released in June 1993, which quickly reached sales of 60,000 plus in the UK and enjoyed a 10-week stay in the Top 75

Below and opposite: Young's European tour with Booker T and the MGs in 1993 won rave reviews and attracted sellout crowds. Grunge stars Pearl Jam guested with them at Finsbury Park

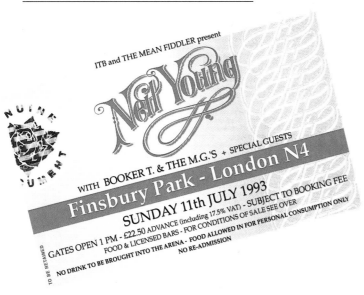

'Like A Hurricane' was seized upon by critics as the highlight of the show, involving as it did the night's most marked transition from electric (as it first appeared on 'American Stars'n'Bars') to acoustic instrumentation. To long-time fans, it might well have pointed up the lack of similarly radical reworkings on offer.

Whatever, it caused the one-time polio patient significant exertion as he pumped energetically with his foot, marginally conserving energy by initially using just his right hand for the famous descending chords. Ducking and diving as he pedalled away, his harmonica coda was particularly eerie over the wheezing organ's howl, an unusual combination of sounds that lent new potency to the plot.

Another Crossroad

An uneventful 'Needle And The Damage Done' followed, before Young looked up once again. 'I'd like to bring on a few of my friends,' he muttered conspiratorially as stepsister Astrid and long-time confederate Nicolette Larson sashayed into the spotlight and took up their positions at the back of the stage, dressed in matching formal black attire. The arrival stage left of Nils Lofgren in bandana and work shirt was many degrees less elegant but more important to the total musical effect.

Lofgren had, by this time, been given his cards by Bruce Springsteen together with the rest of the E Street Band. Neil had helped him re-start his solo career by appearing on his 'Crooked Line' album; now it was time for him to resume his former place. As the girls wailed, Nils contributed unobtrusive but effective accordion to 'Helpless', the night's only nod to Crosby, Stills, Nash and Young, while the title track of 'Harvest Moon' which followed brought an amplified broom to the fore as the shadowy stage was quietly invaded by additional drums, dobro, bass and keyboards.

'Transformer Man' found Nils' voice raised in plaintive support before a pair of country tunes, 'Unknown Legend' (from

'Harvest Moon') and 'Look Out For My Love' (from 'Comes A Time'), dropped the intensity level. 'Long May You Run' brought a knowing smile of triumph from beneath Young's still-furrowed brow before an accordion-laced 'From Hank To Hendrix' took it all home with its 'Marilyn to Madonna, can we get it together?' plea.

It was rare in Young's career for fans to buy two consecutive albums and find music that was remotely similar. And 'Unplugged' certainly reaped the rewards on its release in June 1993: while the rocky live 'Weld' had peaked at Number 15 in Britain and the more laid back acoustic 'Harvest Moon' at Number 9, 'Unplugged' overtook both to reach the Number 4 spot and enjoy a ten-week stay in the charts. Both 'Harvest Moon' and 'Unplugged' were quickly certified silver (60,000 plus sales within the UK). This notably exceeded his Stateside success, where 'Harvest Moon' peaked at Number 16 and 'Unplugged' at 23.

The release of 'Unplugged' was preceded by a curiously timed compilation, 'Lucky Thirteen', which pulled together material from the eclectic career detours he'd made for Geffen in the mid-Eighties. Though Young took a personal hand in its make up, the resulting album remained a hard pill to swallow. It still felt oddly incomplete, and only a liner note from the Loner himself could have placed the music from those strange wilderness years in the context it so desperately needed.

Reviewing it for *Melody Maker*, Allan Jones nailed down the problem when he wrote 'the temptation is to dismiss it out of hand'. But after talking with Young in 1989, he went on to explain that he 'was struck by how much pain they held. These

records are flawed and sometimes paltry, but they tell us a lot about grief and how too much of it can leave us stunned and bewildered, adrift of previously held certainties.'

The way in which 'Lucky Thirteen' was compiled revealed this inner torment. Young had chosen to include an eight-minute alternate take of 'Sample And Hold' from 'Trans', the work he'd recorded to try and come to terms with the awful handicap of cerebral palsy which afflicted both his sons, especially the younger one Ben. The sense of pain was acute, and was further evinced on 'Depression Blues', recorded during his redneck C&W phrase. It oozed with a disgust and disenchantment, sourer than almost anything he'd written.

In the absence of the long-promised 'Decade II/III' (Young was still refining it in 1994) 'Lucky Thirteen' plugged just a tiny proportion of the thousands of gaps for his dedicated followers. A couple of live out-takes from the rockabilly LP, 'Everybody's Rockin'', found their way out of the Broken Arrow bunker, the bitter Bo Diddley-style shuffle of 'Get Gone' and the pained 'Don't Take Your Love From Me'. The maestro also dug out some scuzzier alternate takes from the synthetic lows of 'Landing On Water' and 'Life' which had preceded his electric re-ignition on 'Eldorado'. Of these, the most harrowing was a vastly superior rendering of 'Hippie Dream', the icy, grim stand-out of 'Landing' on which Young let it all hang out in a lather of wrist-slitting despair.

Fortunately he let the listener off the hook by ending the anthology with a brace of upbeat live takes of tracks from 'This Note's For You', the waspish title song and 'Ain't It The Truth', one of those embryonic Young tunes first performed with the

Above: On stage in his native Toronto in 1993

Opposite: Young's appearance at Finsbury Park was considered one of the rock calendar's few worthwhile events of 1993

Squires. All in all, 'Lucky Thirteen' was a bizarre footnote to a body of work that Young still tenaciously defends.

In 1993, Young was, to paraphrase Doug Sahm, 'at another crossroads' of his career. It would have been simple for him to round up the 'Unplugged' mob, go on tour and clean up financially once again. But life for Neil Young was never quite that straightforward. Having enjoyed the blast of playing with them at the Bobfest, he decided to enlist Booker T and the MGs as his backing band and set off on an overseas jaunt.

The pairing was both apposite and inspired: the MGs were the best in the business, and had enjoyed hits in their own right in addition to lending their legendary soulful sound to some of the greatest R&B merchants of all time during their tenure as the Stax/Atlantic house band. Their versatility would be the perfect springboard for the maestro to deliver a set that mixed all the different styles he'd ever played.

By the time the Neil Young roadshow reached North London's Finsbury Park (within spitting distance of the now-derelict Rainbow Theatre where he'd alienated fans with the 'Tonight's The Night' set two decades previously) on Sunday 12 July 1993, the concert had taken on the aura of being one of the rock calendar's few worthwhile events. New media darlings Pearl Jam, Seattle's first supergroup, had been added to the bill – fittingly, since Neil was being heralded as the 'godfather of grunge'! Teenage Fanclub, James and a whole bunch of British kids with guitars that had been but a twinkle in the eyes of mums and dads brought up on 'Heart Of Gold' jockeyed for a chance to be up there treading the boards alongside this truly mythical figure.

Jammin'

Looking chunkier, but the long unkempt hair, four-day stubble and ornate guitar strap as unmistakeable as ever, Young strode on stage and proceeded to lead the MGs on a journey through his past. Stretching back as far as Springfield days and following a long arc that brought things bang up to date with selections from 'Harvest Moon', he even sat down midway through with guitarist Steve Cropper and bassist Donald 'Duck' Dunn for an acoustic break before winding up the set with an old stalwart, 'Down By The River'. The choice of encores was telling: having introduced Booker T and Company individually, he offered '(Sittin' On) The Dock Of The Bay', a personal tribute to the late, great Otis Redding whose hits the MGs had graced.

With a laconic, 'This is a song for my old friend, Bob,' he then launched into emotional 'All Along The Watchtower', still as much Hendrix as Dylan, and logged out with the obligatory Nineties anthem, 'Rockin' In The Free World', for which he was eagerly joined by members of Pearl Jam. It was a passionate couple of hours – a historic performance that had magically vanquished the drizzle threatening to dampen the fun as the

set began, and one that had put fire in the bones of 20,000 chilled but dedicated fans.

After the tour, studio sessions with the MGs were booked, but cancelled when Dunn was diagnosed as suffering from throat cancer. Young considered summoning Sonic Youth, which would have been an unearthly but inspired marriage – but instead Crazy Horse were brought out of stud and work began on Young's latest opus. Songs like the divinely titled 'Piece Of Crap' and 'Gone To Hell' marked a return to the frantic guitar maelstroms of 'Rust' and 'Ragged Glory'.

They also laid down 'Blue Horse' and 'Change Your Mind', two new songs aired at Finsbury Park. But the whole project was almost derailed in March 1994 when Billy Talbot reputedly leaked details of these activities to staunch Young fan and collector Bill Ryan, who had been staying at the bass player's Californian home.

Ryan, *Melody Maker* reported, tried to convince Talbot to let him have the studio masters of songs that Neil and the Horse had recorded together the previous December. The bass player allegedly handed over to Ryan a handwritten record of song titles and lyrics from the work in progress, which was then circulated to bootleggers. Ryan also claimed that he had on tape several hours of material from these same sessions.

Photographer Joel Bernstein, who also acts as Neil Young's official archivist and guitar tuner, picked up on this on Internet, an electronic noticeboard accessible to the general public. He reported back to Elliot Roberts, Young's long-time manager, and the shit hit the proverbial fan. While unofficial bootlegging for private consumption is widespread among obsessional aficionados of many acts (and Young's dedicated

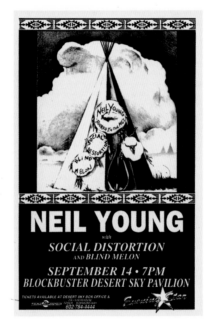

followers are no different), the singer had always jealously guarded all his recordings, and was notorious for maintaining total control of their use – hence his avowed disinterest in a Buffalo Springfield boxed set then being compiled by those outside his jurisdiction.

He clearly regarded the affair as a breach of trust, and one that threatened to destroy once and for all his quarter-century relationship with the legendary band. Happily, Talbot and the singer resolved their differences and Young and Crazy Horse's volatile union survived to see another day.

If this domestic glitch had kicked off 1994 on a jumpy note, the drug-derived death of Nirvana singer Kurt Cobain in April placed it on an altogether more sinister footing. Cobain had paid lip service to Young's strong influence in the creation of his band's guitar sound, but Kurt went one bizarre step further when he quoted the famous line from 'Hey Hey My My' (Into The Black)' – 'It's better to burn out than to fade away' – in his suicide note.

This must inevitably have re-opened some of the old wounds caused by Danny Whitten and Bruce Berry's own deaths and made Young feel that rock'n'roll never learns from its mistakes. The same squalid excesses that had killed two of his closest friends had now claimed yet another victim. The connection was not lost on Pearl Jam singer Eddie Vedder, whose group had enjoyed a friendly rivalry with Nirvana. Playing emotional shows in New York immediately after Cobain's death, a grieving Vedder slipped in a series of musical references, notably on 'Daughter', which ended with him one night fading out with a quote from 'Hey Hey My My' and, on another, breaking into an improvised rendition of 'Tonight's The Night'.

No Let-Up

While Young was putting the finishes touches to his latest album with Crazy Horse 'Sleeps With Angels' (the title track a tribute to the late Cobain),which was released in September 1994, Messrs Molina and Talbot moonlighted with ex-Icicle Works supremo Ian McNabb, playing on one half of his This Way Up album 'Head Like A Rock' and performing some live dates including a showcase at the Glastonbury Festival. McNabb had never been afraid to reveal his obsession with Neil's music and the band at times sounded frighteningly like Young and Crazy Horse.

Acclaimed by some critics one of Young greatest work in recent years, 'Sleeps With Angels' was a return to the dark tone of 'Tonight's The Night' and 'Zuma'. Among its 12 tracks, a mixture of 'rockers and ballads', it features an epic 15-minute work-out entitled 'Change Your Mind' overloaded with guitar

1993 saw Young being heralded as the 'godfather of grunge' and appearing live with bands such as Social Distortion and Pearl Jam (at the MTV Awards, above)

solos. The much-anticipated 'Piece Of Crap' on the other hand packs all the bite of 'This Note's For You', a strident anti-materialist consumer diatribe that, in the words of a *Melody Maker* preview, reports what happened 'when you buy something through mail-order, it turns up – and it's a piece of crap.'

For nearly 30 years now, Neil Young has been confounding his public's expectations, railing at an industry he openly despises and chiselling out a position in rock'n'roll's shrinking pantheon second only to his hero, Bob Dylan. He steadfastly refuses to grow old gracefully – and, as he once affirmed to *Melody Maker*:

'When I go, I'm gonna go fighting. That's for sure.'

This Note's For You
(Neil Young & the Blue Notes) (1988)

Young here tipped his fedora to masters of the blues like Muddy Waters and BB King and reincarnated himself as Shakey Deal, a late-Eighties Blues Brothers lookalike! 'This Note's For You' found him in fine guitar-playing and vocal shape, fronting a 10-piece swing band with no less than six horn players.

After the indulgences of the Geffen years, this latest work caught him with renewed vigour and purpose – he actually sounded as if he meant it and the grooves were alive with joie de vivre, this being in no small way unrelated to his much-heralded return to the Reprise label.

While in no respect vintage Young, 'This Note's For You' scored high on the enjoyment factor and, more importantly, signalled the first stage in the singer's late-Eighties' artistic renaissance.

Track Listing:

Ten Men Workin' • This Note's For You • Coupe De Ville • Life In The City • Twilight • Married Man • Sunny Inside • Can't Believe Your Lyin' • Hey Hey • One Thing

American Dream
(with Crosby, Stills & Nash) (1988)

Young took the upper hand in this belated CSN&Y reunion and in addition to two he co-wrote with Stills, contributed a further four solo songs, arguably some of the album's best. While the title cut, stylistically not too far removed from 'Landing On Water', only came alive on the scorching Young guitar solo, 'Feel Your Love' was a real bonus, a practically solo acoustic ballad that could have fallen off the sessions for 'Harvest' or 'After The Goldrush'. Best of all was 'This Old House' that lyrically seemed a riposte to the 'Our House' song Graham Nash had written for 'Déjà Vu', the optimism of which was here replaced by a tone of failure. For CS&N 'American Dream' might have signalled an upturn in careers that had been marking time. For Young it was nothing more than a distraction – he had bigger and better fish to fry!

Track Listing:

American Dream • Got It Made • Name Of Love • Don't Say Goodbye • This Old House • Nighttime For The Generals • Shadowland • Drivin' Thunder • Clear Blue Skies • That Girl • Compass • Soldiers Of Peace • Feel Your Love • Night Song

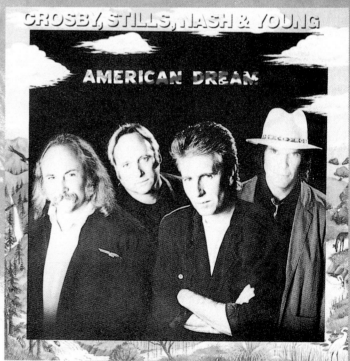

Freedom
(Neil Young & the Restless)   (1989)

Although as happy as a mudlark with the Blue Notes, Young suddenly booked himself into New York's Hit Factory at the end of 1988, and recorded some of the most gut-wrenching heavy-rock guitar workouts of his career. But these sessions, tentatively called 'Times Square', were never released. A taster, a five-track EP 'Eldorado' (also a later name for these same sessions), was issued in Australia and Japan. Instead Young decided to put out the hour-long 'Freedom', a master-work that culled material from 'Times Square', 'Eldorado', the Blue Notes and new tracks with Linda Ronstadt. It confirmed that Young's 'second coming' was at hand.

'Freedom's undoubted highlight was 'Rockin' In The Free World', which was seized upon by many experiencing for the first time a 'free' society in the wake of the fall of the Soviet Union and the tearing down of the Berlin Wall.

Track Listing:

Rockin' In The Free World • Crime In The City (Sixty To Zero Part 1) • Don't Cry • Hangin' On A Limb • Eldorado • The Ways Of Love • Someday • On Broadway • Wrecking Ball • Too Far Gone • Rockin' In The Free World

Ragged Glory
(Neil Young & Crazy Horse)   (1990)

With 'Ragged Glory' Neil Young was clearly on a roll, as he re-assembled the team of Crazy Horse and producer David Briggs. The album was recorded in one major creative burst at the Broken Arrow ranch and exorcised all the negativity that had killed off his last two collaborations with Messrs Talbot, Molina and Sampedro. The long closing cut 'Mother Earth (Natural Anthem)', recorded at the Hoosier Dome Farm Aid gig was Young seemingly looking back at hippie days through rose-tinted shades – as in 'Mansion On The Hill' he seemed to be taking shelter in those halcyon days.

But the real delight of 'Ragged Glory' with all its shit-kickin' back to basics garage rock was to see its creator seize victory from the jaws of defeat – in his disillusionment with the present, he had found salvation in the life-asserting guitar duels with Crazy Horse.

Track Listing

Country Home • White Line • F*!#in' Up • Over And Over • Love To Burn • Farmer John • Mansion On The Hill • Days That Used To Be • Love And Only Love • Mother Earth (Natural Anthem)

Weld

(Neil Young & Crazy Horse)   (1991)

'Weld' was the soundtrack to the Gulf War, a work that echoed in every groove the death, pain and hell of war. Recorded on the 'Smell The Horse' tour, Young threw out selections from the last album to make room for old songs that fitted the mood – 'Cortez The Killer', 'Powderfinger', and most powerful of all Dylan's 'Blowin' In The Wind', played at funereal pace with screaming feedback and flame-thrower guitars. The double set came with a limited edition third disc, 'Arc', a 35-minutes of sequences of music randomly taken from the beginnings and ends of live performances and welded together to create a viscous continuous cycle of guitar noise. It was one of Young's greatest innovations to date.

Track Listing:

Hey Hey My My (Into The Black) • Crime In The City • Blowin' In The Wind • Welfare Mothers • Love To Burn • Cinnamon Girl • Mansion On The Hill • F*#!in' Up • Cortez The Killer • Powderfinger • Love And Only Love • Rockin' In The Free World • Like A Hurricane • Farmer John • Tonight's The Night • Roll Another Number

Harvest Moon   (1992)

Having taken his electric escapades just about as far as he could, Young solved the question of where to go next by making the album fans had been pestering him to make for 20 years. Although he was loath to acknowledge it as such, he assembled the same musicians (the Stray Gators and Linda Ronstadt) and even christened it 'Harvest Moon'. Stylistically it lay somewhere between its 1972 predecessor and the gentle, folksy 'Comes A Time' from 1978 (the presence of Nicolette Larson a connecting thread). If it musically nodded its head back to the sound of the early Seventies, its sense of nostalgia was compounded by its central concerns, which revolved around the idea of loss and the need to go on. 'Harvest Moon' saw Young back on the porch, softly strumming his acoustic guitar, full of introspection. But the fans got what they wanted, and they gave him his best-selling album to date.

Track Listing:

Unknown Legend • From Hank To Hendrix • You And Me • Harvest Moon • War Of Man • One Of These Days • Such A Woman • Old King • Dreamin' Man • Natural Beauty

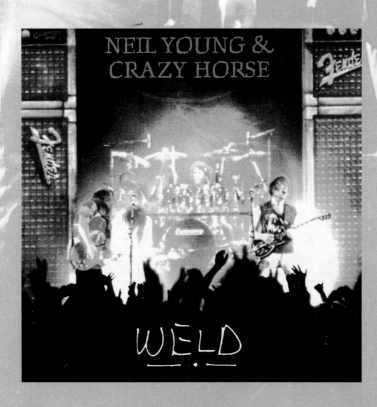

Lucky Thirteen (1993)

Released long after Young had left the Geffen label, but reputedly compiled by his guiding hand, 'Lucky Thirteen' was a belated attempt to put the wilderness years, 1982-87, into some kind of perspective.

Much of the material consisted of out-takes unreleased songs; there was 'Depression Blues', once intended for the aborted Farm Aid EP, live tunes written at the same time as the rockabilly tribute 'Everybody's Rockin', even a glimpse of how the sessions for 'Landing On Water' and 'Life' should have sounded. As if to ram home his sense of despair, he chose to include an alternate cut of 'Hippie Dream'. The album ended on a surprising upbeat tone with two songs associated with the Blue Notes – 'Ain't It The Truth' (from his Squires days) and an alternate 'This Note's For You', the title cut of the album which marked his return to Reprise.

Track Listing:

Sample And Hold • Transformer Man • Depression Blues • Get Gone • Don't Take Your Love Away From Me • Once An Angel • Where Is The Highway Tonight • Hippie Dream • Pressure • Around The World • Mideast Vacation • Ain't It The Truth • This Note's For You

Unplugged (1993)

By reaching Number 4 in Britain, this spinoff of his MTV appearance gave Neil Young his most successful album since 'Harvest', and one that eclipsed even 'After The Goldrush'. 'Stringman' appeared on record for the first time, but most notable about the track listing was what Young chose not to play: 'Goldrush', 'Heart Of Gold', 'Old Man', even 'Sugar Mountain' were absent, though the selection was spiced by a sample apiece from the Springfield and CSN&Y songbooks.

An overhauled 'Like A Hurricane' was played effectively on pump organ, but elsewhere the sound was very familiar – unlike, say, Nirvana whose unplugged set would emerge as radically different in sound to their electrified selves. Despite his sniping at MTV, Young had condescended to play their game, in the process revealing little his audience hadn't already guessed.

Track Listing:

The Old Laughing Lady • Mr Soul • World On A String • Pocahontas • Stringman • Like A Hurricane • The Needle And The Damage Done • Helpless • Harvest Moon • Transformer Man • Unknown Legend • Look Out For My Love • Long May You Run • From Hank To Hendrix

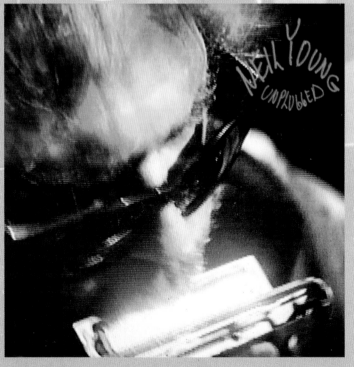

Photographic acknowledgments

Canapress /Blaise Edwards 129;

© 1967 Bill Graham #98. Artists, Kelly & Stanley Mouse 27;

© 1968 Bill Graham #122. Artist Lee Conkin 32;

John Einarson Collection 10, 13, 14, 17, 21, /Mrs Liz Clark and Jack Harper 20 top, 20 bottom;

Michael Heatley/Atlantic Records 74 right, Geffen Records 155 right, 156 left, 156 right, 157 left, /Reprise Records 74 left, 75 left, 77 right, 114, 115 left, 116 left, 117 left, 117 right, 118 right, 119 left, 119 right, 154 right, 188 left;

Alan Jenkins 21, 31, 34, 63,150,160 left, 160 right, 174, 182 bottom, 183, 186, /Atlantic Records 29, 30, 33, 35, 38 right, 39 left, 39 right, 54, 55, 67, 75 right, 76 right, 115 right, 188 right, /Steve Babineau 180, /Jeff Blake 184, /Peter Doherty 152, 153, /Geffen Records 157 right, 191 left, /1990 Salvatore di Giacomo 134, /Reprise Records 46, 47, 50, 59, 70, 72, 76 left, 77 left, 82, 86, 94, 97, 98, 101, 103, 104, 116 right, 118 left, 155 left, 167, 189 left, 189 right, 190 left, 190 right, 191 right, /United Artists 102, /WEA Music 182 top, /Mark Webber 19;

London Features International front flap bottom, 11, 12, 18, 79, 80, 95, 106- 107, 114-115, 159, /R J Capak 125, /Robin Kaplan 149, /Michael Ochs back jacket bottom, front flap top, back flap top, 36, 37, 40, 69, 74-75, 76-77, /Neal Preston /Andy Kent back flap bottom, /Michael Putland 84, 88, /Ebet Roberts 100, 154-155, 172, /Ken Regan 142;

Melody Maker 104, 111, 128, /Richard E Aaron 99, /Ian Astle 175, /Andrew Catlin © 1990 165, /Robert Ellis 42, 52-53, 60, 78, /Frontline Pictures 58, /Steve Gullick 185, 188-189, /Chris Horler 85, 96, /PicturePower 8, /Neal Preston 112-113, 118-119, /Tom Sheehan front cover, back jacket top, 1, 136, 140, 145, 164, /SKR Photos 45, /Stephen Sweet 7, 168, /Matthew Taylor 93;

Pictorial Press 90, 91, 161, 179, /Star File/Dagmar 89;

Redferns /Richie Aaron 109, /Glenn A Baker Archives 23 top, 28 top, /Dick Barnatt 56, 61, 64-65, 73, /David Ellis 102-103, /Barry Levine 51, /Stephen Morley 87, 106 inset, 110-111, 116-117, 122-23, 135, /NE/Volker Jensen 151, /David Redfern 23 inset, /Ebet Roberts 6 bottom , 143, 148, 177, /Bob Willoughby 26, 28 bottom, 110, /Val Wilmer 24;

Relay Photos 41, 49, 57, 66, /Andre Csillag 105, 124, /David Wainwright 127, /Chris Walters 83;

Reprise Records 44;

Retna Pictures Ltd 81, /Ross Barnett 126, /Jay Blakesberg 162-163, /Armando Gallo front flap, centre, /Gary Gershoff 9 right, 131, /Beth Gwinn 138, /Andrea Laubach 139, 146-147,141 right, /David Peterson back flap centre, /Michael Putland 9 inset, /Steve Rapport 170-171, /Joseph Sia 121, /Peter Tangen 158, /Jeff Tisman 190-191, /Luciano Viti cover spine;

Rex Features 120, 132, 133, /Nick Elgar 144, /Dave Hogan 187, /LGI /Chris Kehoe 6 top, /LGI/David M Warren 88, 166;

Western Canada Pictorial Index 15;

Winnipeg Free Press 16.